D1605534

BISTRO COOKING
with jeanette

Food styling by Jeanette Nuss and Patricia Monda
Photographs by Patricia Monda

Dennis Happy Cooking Jeanette 10-26-04

For orders contact Publisher
Jeanette Mansour Nuss
P.O. Box 284
Lincoln, California 95648

www.bistrocookbook.com

ISBN 0-9726174-9-3

First Edition

10 9 8 7 6 5 4 3 2 1

ACKNOWLEDGEMENT

My gratitude is endless. I happen to be the luckiest person in the world. I cannot express my million thanks to all the people who got involved. First I would like to thank my family for being supportive in this project when so many times I have almost given up. Fred, my husband who stood beside me and encouraged me through all the phases of this book. Chad, my son, you are an inspiration to me, and you and Holly have been instrumental in the creation of this book. Chad and Holly, your persistence in asking me "when are you going to write this cookbook" finally paid off, here it is. This cookbook has been published several times in my imagination and only once in print.

Thank you to my good friend Pat Monda who is the photographer for *Bistro Cooking with jeanette.* I recall the photo shoots we did, scrambling through our closets, borrowing serving platters from everyone we could find. Also the creative energy that both of us put forth together in getting the final touches just right. All the off-roading, discovering farms, groves and orchards, the many farmer's markets in 100 degree weather.

To Angela Blas, my formatting Angel, who rescued me many times arguing with my computer. My car drove itself on automatic directly to your house. To Joan Logue, Agnes Valdez, Carole McGovern, Margaret Guiler, Sue McPherson, my Elf Angels, the editors that just would not give up, and getting this book to where it needed to be. Joan Logue, thanks for all the hours editing and talking to the computers, and the great laughs we had. Thanks to Del Webb for the computer lab, now I have my own computer. To Margaret Guiler who is a very good friend. The Kauai long distance editor. The daily emails helping me to name this book, all the advice and sharing of good and bad days together. To Sue McPherson, the Big Bear Lake editor. Her knowledge of food and recipes is incredible. We shared plenty of good times. To Lily Hazbun, my sister, one of the greatest accomplished cooks on this earth, thank you for your support and the daily phone conversations.

CREDITS

Crate and Barrel
Melissa Ferrari
Lily and Albert Hazbun
Noral and Keith Prouhet
Twin Peaks Orchards
Brennan Peach Orchards
Chad and Holly Nuss
Brian and Lori Nuss
Pat and Lew Monda
Salle Orchards
Dick Kettel

INTRODUCTION

Bistro cooking has been inspired by my travels both on the road and in my culinary imaginations. It is an infusion of cultures and traditions and my passion for food. I recall the many get-togethers with my family, especially my grandmother who took the role of my mother who died at an early age. My grandmother was an accomplished cook. Our house was always filled with amazing smells that tempted our friends to share our meals. Morning, noon, or night there was always something cooking on the stove or in the oven. I will never forget those distinct smells and flavors.

Bistro Cooking with jeanette is a style of cooking that is mixed with these memorable flavors and taste. It is a rustic type of cuisine that invokes the senses. Bistro cooking is reflective and soul satisfying, a very informal type of cooking where friends and family are invited to dinner for no specific reason ... maybe because you want to share.

I have placed a great emphasis on fresh, earthy ingredients that burst with smell and flavors of hearty scented stews, bubbly au gratins, aromatic soups, simple mouth watering desserts. Nothing is better than preparing a family style meal as your home fills with an aromatic orchestra of flavors.

The main bistro of my life is within my own home. Homey, humble and jovial, these characteristics translate quickly to the foods that I have created, and the foods that you will soon learn to prepare. Bistro is a way of life, and I believe that sharing my culinary and family experiences will enable you to share your bistro cooking with others. With a collection of over 120 recipes and 75 color photos that will inspire you and those around you to enjoy the home bistro for themselves.

Joyeux Cuisine!

Jeanette Mansour Nuss

Jeanette Mansour Nuss

CONTENTS

COOKING TERMS

Al Dente: In Italian it means "to the tooth". Slightly firm, not soft or mushy.

Au Gratin: A combination of ingredients cooked in a casserole topped with bread crumbs and cheese and browned in the oven or broiler.

Au Jus: Served with its own juices.

Bain-Marie: A water bath, whereas a container is placed inside, or over a second container filled with hot water. Commonly used for cooking food surrounded with simmering water.

Bake: A process of cooking in the oven where raw ingredients are surrounded by hot air.

Baste: To moisten foods during cooking with pan drippings or special sauce to add flavors and prevent drying.

Blanch: To immerse in rapidly boiling water and allow to cook slightly.

Boil: When raw ingredients are cooked in water (or other liquid). The liquid that is bubbling rapidly. Rapid boil is when it breaks the surface waves. Full rolling boil liquid that rises to the surface and tumbles into waves.

Bouquet Garni: Usually when several herbs and spices are gathered together and assembled in a cheese cloth tied like a bundle. It is used in soups, stews, stocks.

Butterfly: To make several shallow slices on meat or poultry. Do not cut all the way through. Spread open.

Braise: A cooking technique where the raw ingredients are usually seared in fat and then tightly covered and cooked with the addition of some liquid.

Broil: When ingredients are cooked with radiant heat from above, usually with a gas flame or an electric element.

Caramelize: The browning of sugar. Also applies to sautéing ingredients until brown in color and resembles caramel.

Chiffonade: Is the technique of stacking leaves flat, rolling into a jellyroll, and thinly sliced.

Clarified Butter: Butter from which milk solids and water have been removed leaving pure butterfat. To achieve clarified butter: Place butter in a saucepan, heat on high. When butter starts bubbling, remove from heat. Skim off the foam from top. Let stand. Slowly pour clear butter. Do not disturb bottom of pan.

Créme Fraîche: A cream resembling sour cream that has a tangy flavor. It is quite rich tasting.

Deglaze: To dissolve cooked particles in a small amount of liquid by swirling and scraping drippings.

Fold: To incorporate a delicate substance, such as whipped cream or beaten egg whites, into another substance without releasing air bubbles. A spatula is used to gently bring part of the mixture from the bottom of the bowl to the top. The process is repeated, while slowly rotating the bowl, until the ingredients are thoroughly blended.

Glaze: To cover with a glossy coating, such as gelatin, or jelly for fruit desserts. For meat, to coat with a sauce and brown it in an oven.

Grill: A cooking technique where a raw ingredient is placed on a open grid over a radiant heat ource.

Julienne: To cut vegetables, fruits or cheeses into match sticks slivers.

Macerate: The act of soaking a food in a liquid to incorporate the flavors. Usually used for fruits.

Marinate: Preparation technique where food is soaked in a seasoned liquid, usually for the purpose of flavoring or tenderizing.

Melon Baller: A small hand tool whose curved, cup-shaved blade is used for cutting fruits, vegetables, and other soft fleshed food into balls.

Parboil: To boil until partially cooked – to blanch. Usually this procedure is followed by final cooking in a seasoned sauce.

Poach: To cook very gently in hot liquid kept just below the boiling point.

Puree: When food has been finely mashed and or strained to a thick, smooth pulp-like consistency.

Reduce: A cooking technique where a liquid is boiled rapidly until the quantity is decreased to a desired consistency by evaporation. The result is concentration of flavors.

Roast: Cooking technique when raw ingredients are cooked in an oven

Roux: Is a paste mixture of butter and flour cooked together to use as a thickening agent.

Sauté: Comes from a French word meaning "to jump". It is the process of cooking or browning food in a small quantity of hot oil.

Simmer: To cook in liquid just below the boiling point. The surface of the liquid should be barely moving, broken from time to time by slowly rising bubbles.

Steep: To let food stand in hot liquid to extract or to enhace flavor.

Steam: When food is cooked directly or indirectly by the steam created from boiling water or other liquids.

Sweat: When food is cooked and releases moisture.

Toss: To combine ingredients with a lifting motion.

Chicken Lettuce Cupette, recipe on page 10.

Pâté Maison Jeanette, recipe on page 11.

APPETIZERS

CHICKEN LETTUCE CUPETTE

Great recipe for lunch or dinner. One of my favorite recipes. Garlic chili sauce can be purchased in the oriental section of most supermarkets.

Prep time: 20 min. Cook time: 20 min. Makes 32 cupettes

Ingredients:

1 large	head Boston lettuce leaves, separated, washed and dried
1 large	head radicchio, separated, washed and dried
2 tablespoons	olive oil
1 pound	ground chicken <u>or</u> turkey
1 medium	yellow pepper, seeded, veins removed and diced
1 medium	red pepper, seeded, veins removed and diced
1/2 cup	basil leaves, chopped
2 tablespoons	Worcestershire sauce
1 medium	lime, juiced
2 cloves	garlic, peeled and crushed
1 small	jalapeno chili, seeded, veins removed and diced
1 teaspoon	granulated sugar
1 teaspoon	garlic chili sauce

Topping:

1 cup	pistachio nuts, chopped
1/2 bunch	green onions (scallions) trimmed and sliced.

Tear leaves of lettuce and radicchio into approximately 3x3 inch pieces and set aside.

Heat olive oil in a sauté pan, add ground chicken and all remaining ingredients. Mix together, and cook over medium heat until chicken is cooked through.

To serve: Place one tablespoon of the mixture on each lettuce and radicchio leaf forming a cup shape. Top with sliced green onions (scallions) and chopped pistachio nuts.

See photo on page 8

PÂTÉ MAISON JEANETTE

Great recipe to assemble and freeze prior to serving. Can cook one loaf for immediate serving, and freeze the extra one. If you are creative you can garnish the top of the glazing with herbs and vegetables, making an artistic design.

Prep time: 40 min. Cook time: 1 hr. Makes 2 loaf pans (8-1/2 x 4-1/2 x 2-3/4)

Preheat oven to 375°

Ingredients:

1 pound	salt pork
1 pound	ground chicken
1 pound	ground veal
2 beaten	egg yolks
1 cup	heavy cream

Marinade:

1 cup	cherry brandy
2 dried	bay leaves
1 teaspoon	poultry seasoning

Glazing:

4 envelopes	unflavored gelatin
2 tablespoons	cognac
2 (14 ounce)	cans beef or chicken broth

Garnish: fresh rosemary or cut up vegetables.

Remove rind from salt pork and cut pork into one-inch cubes. Place in a pan of water, cover and bring to a boil. Boil for three minutes and drain. Mix marinade together and pour over salt pork, ground chicken and veal. Cover and keep in refrigerator until ready to use. Drain meats, reserving 1/4 cup marinade.

Using the food processor with a steel blade, chop meat to puree consistency. Place in mixing bowl. Add beaten egg yolks, 1/4 cup reserved marinade and mix together. Whip cream and fold into meat mixture. Place in 2 loaf pans.

Place in a Bain Marie (water bath, see cooking terms) and bake for one hour. Test by inserting a toothpick into the meat. Make sure juices are clear, not red. Remove pâté from oven, drain fat and let stand for two hours at room temperature. Loosen loaves with knife, if needed. Unmold.

For glazing, soften gelatin in warm broth. Add cognac and stir together. Spray or oil loaf pan and line with enough plastic wrap to fit bottom, sides and top. Pour in one inch of the glazing. Let chill until gelatin is set. Garnish top of glazing with herbs or cut up vegetables. Place pâté on top. Pour remaining glazing on pâté. Cover and chill.

To unmold, turn pâté on a platter, remove plastic wrap, garnish with rosemary and serve with crackers, cornichons and Dijon mustard.

See photo on page 8

PEACHES GORGONZOLA BRUSCHETTA

This recipe is great to serve after dinner. Also, you can substitute any seasonal fruits. Figs are an excellent choice.

Prep time: 20 min. Makes 6 servings

Ingredients:

6 ounces	Gorgonzola cheese
2 tablespoons	extra virgin olive oil
6 slices	French bread, cut 1/2 inch thick
2 large	ripe fresh peaches, unpeeled
Garnish:	several basil leaves

Place Gorgonzola cheese and olive oil in food processor, process until smooth. Spread the mixture on the slices of French bread.

Cut peaches in half. Separate each peach from its pit by gently twisting the halves in opposite directions. Slice peaches vertically into 1/4 inch slices. Place 4 slices of peaches on each piece of the prepared sliced bread. Garnish with fresh leaves of basil.

Serve immediately. Enjoy!

TURKEY BUNDLES

This recipe can be used with ham or roast beef slices instead of turkey. A great do ahead recipe. After assembling bundles, wrap them tightly with plastic wrap.

Prep time: 45 min. Makes 40 rolls

Ingredients:

12 ounces	smoked turkey, thinly sliced, cut 2x4 inch each
6 ounces	chèvre (goat cheese)
2 tablespoons	basil leaves, chopped
1 medium	yellow pepper, seeded, sliced into 3 inch julienne strips
1 medium	red pepper, seeded, sliced into 3 inch julienne strips
1 bunch	chives for garnish

Mix chèvre with chopped basil. Spread a thin layer of chèvre mixture on each turkey slice.

Lay one strip each of yellow and red julienne pepper across the 2-inch width of sliced turkey.

Roll securely, arrange on a tray seam side down and secure each with a toothpick.

Cover tightly with plastic wrap. Refrigerate until ready to serve. Garnish by tying each bundle with a chive.

ROQUEFORT PEAR FEUILLETTE

If working with phyllo makes you uneasy, I suggest purchasing the mini Fillo Dough Shells. Usually I keep the shells in the freezer. When making the filling, double the recipe and freeze the excess. It is a lifesaver appetizer when expecting company. You can fill the frozen shells with filling and freeze. Cover well with aluminum foil and bake for just 8 minutes.

Prep time: 35 min. Cook time: 25-35 min. Makes 30 pieces using phyllo dough

Prep time: 10 min. Cook time: 5 min.

Makes 30 ready made, fully baked, mini Fillo Dough Shells

Preheat oven to 350°

Ingredients:

Syrup Ingredients:

1 cup	water
3/4 cup	sugar
1 tablespoon	rosewater <u>or</u> 1 teaspoon vanilla
2 large	pears, peeled and diced into 1/4 inch pieces
3.5 ounces	Roquefort cheese, crumbled
1 pound	butter, clarified
1 pound	phyllo dough <u>or</u> 2 packages of ready made, fully baked mini Fillo Dough Shells
Garnish:	bunch of chives (tie bundles prior to serving)

Mix water, sugar, rosewater or vanilla in a pan. Then place peeled and diced pears into pan with syrup. Cook over low heat until tender. Drain and mix in crumbled Roquefort cheese. Set aside.

Clarify butter (see cooking terms). Place phyllo sheets on a moist towel. Cover with plastic wrap and top with a moist towel until ready to use. Uncover phyllo sheets. Use a 6 inch round plate as a pattern to cut the phyllo sheets into round circles. Place the plate on top of the phyllo as close to both edges as possible, since you want to repeat this process twice. The bottom part will be used for the 3x3 inch square pieces. Using a sharp knife cut around the plate making sure you cut the circle all the way through the sheets of phyllo. Repeat the process twice, totaling three stacks of 6-inch circles. Cover with moist towel and set aside. Cut 3x3 inch squares out of the remaining uncut phyllo and repeat twice, totaling 3 stacks of 3x3 inches squares. Cover and set aside.

Spray or butter mini muffin pans. Take 2 circles of phyllo, brush with clarified butter and place in mini muffin pan. Butter two 3x3 inch squares of phyllo and gently place them into the mini muffin pan on top of the circles. Make a well in the center. Fill with 1/2 teaspoon Roquefort cheese and poached pear mixture, repeat procedure to do the remaining bundles. Close the dough to make a pouch or bundle over the filling. Tie loosely with string. Brush with butter. Repeat until all circles are done. Bake in a preheated oven for 25 minutes or until light brown.

When bundles are cooled, remove strings and tie with chives prior to serving. These bundles can be done ahead of time and frozen. They need not be defrosted before reheating.

If using the pre-baked shells, fill with 1 teaspoon of Roquefort cheese and pear mixture, gently brush top and sides with butter. Place in mini muffin pans and bake at 375 degrees for 5 minutes. Store per package directions.

See photo on page 16

CRUSTLESS QUICHETTE

These quichettes can be cooked in a quiche pan and served for lunch, accompanied by a salad.

Prep time: 25 min. Cook time: 20 min. Makes 72 mini quiches

Preheat oven to 400°

Ingredients:

5 large	eggs, beaten
1/2 teaspoon	baking soda
1/2 teaspoon	baking powder
1/4 cup	olive oil
1/2 cup	unbleached flour
1 (4 ounce)	can mild diced green chilies, drained
1 (4 ounce)	jar diced pimiento, drained
3/4 cup	ricotta or cottage cheese
3/4 cup	Swiss cheese, grated
1/2 cup	mozzarella cheese, grated
1 (4.25 ounce)	can black olives, drained and chopped
1/2 teaspoon	cumin
1/2 bunch	cilantro, stems removed, washed, dried and chopped
salt and pepper	to taste
couple of drops	of Tabasco sauce (optional)

Garnish:

2 tablespoons	sour cream
2 tablespoons	black olives, chopped
2 tablespoons	red pepper, chopped
72 leaves	cilantro

Prepare mini-muffin pans by spraying with olive oil spray and dust with corn meal, shake off excess.

In a bowl, place beaten eggs. Add baking soda, baking powder, olive oil, flour, chilies, pimiento, and mix together. Add in ricotta or cottage cheese, Swiss cheese, mozzarella cheese, chopped black olives, cumin, cilantro, salt and pepper, Tabasco sauce and mix together well. Fill prepared mini pans 3/4 full. Bake for 10 minutes at 400 degrees. Reduce heat to 350 degrees. Bake for 10 minutes or until a toothpick comes out clean. Remove from oven, cool and invert on a rack.

Garnish by placing a little sour cream in center of each quichette and top with chopped black olives, chopped red pepper, and one cilantro leaf.

Leftover cooked quichettes can be frozen and reheated for 2 minutes on high in the microwave, or 10-15 minutes in the oven.

See photo on page 16

Roquefort Pear Feuillette see recipe on page 14.

Crustless Quichette see recipe on page 15.

Spinach Phyllo Logs see recipe on page 23.

Kibbee Croquette see recipe on page 19.

Hummus Bi Tahini see recipe on page 170.

Eggplant or Zucchini Tahini Puree see recipe on page 18.

EGGPLANT OR ZUCCHINI TAHINI PUREE
BABA GHANNOUJ

Tahini is a thick oily paste of ground sesame seeds used in Middle Eastern cooking. Tahini can be purchased in cans or jars. It is sold in most supermarkets and health food stores. When using Tahini, stir it in the jar or can prior to measuring. Make sure it is refrigerated after opening the jar. Baba Ghannouj is an excellent accompaniment to grilled chicken, fish or any meat.

Prep time: 20 min. Cook time: 1 hr. 20 min. Serves 6-8

Preheat oven at 400°

Ingredients:

2 large	eggplants, or 6 medium zucchini, trimmed
2 cloves	garlic, peeled and crushed
4 tablespoons	Tahini (sesame paste)
1/4 cup	lemon juice
1/4 cup	lime juice
salt and pepper	to taste

Garnish:

1 tablespoon	olive oil
2 tablespoons	chopped parsley

Pierce the eggplants with a fork. Place eggplants or zucchini on a baking sheet. Bake until quite soft, and shrunken in size.

Remove from the heat and place in a bowl to cool. Save juices from eggplants or zucchini. Peel eggplants. (If using zucchini, do not peel). Place in the food processor along with the remaining ingredients and process until a smooth puree consistency.

Place on a serving platter. Top with olive oil and chopped parsley. Serve with slices of pita bread.

See photo on page 17

KIBBEE CROQUETTE

This dish is renowned among Middle Eastern dishes. The word Kibbee comes from the verb that means "to form into a ball." Basic ingredients for Kibbee are bulgur, or crushed wheat, and meat. It can be served as an appetizer or an entrée.

Prep time: 10 min. Cook time: 25 min. Makes 20-24

Preheat oven at 400°

Ingredients:

3/4 cup	bulgur (cracked wheat)
1 large	onion, peeled and cut into 1/2 inch pieces
1 teaspoon	salt
1/2 teaspoon	allspice
3/4 pound	ground lean lamb, beef, chicken, or turkey
3 tablespoons	vegetable oil

Cover bulgur with cold water, soak for 10 minutes. Drain and press between palms of hand to remove excess water.

Place cut onion in food processor and process until pureed. Along with the pureed onion, add drained bulgur, ground meat, salt, pepper and allspice into the bowl of the food processor. Process together until mixture is a paste-like consistency. Remove mixture and place in a bowl.

Dip hands in ice water and divide the mixture into 20-24 balls. Roll to shape into corks, balls or egg shapes. Generously oil a baking sheet, roll each croquette in oil to coat all sides.

Bake at 400 degrees for 14 minutes. Turn croquettes over and cook for another 10 minutes.

Serve with Yogurt Pine Nut Sauce (see recipe in sauce section).

See photo on page 17

SALMON FLEURETTE WITH CARAMELIZED BELGIAN ENDIVE

Great recipe to do ahead. Caramelize endive. Assemble salmon with dressing. Let stand until ready to assemble.

Prep time: 10 min. Cook time: 15 min. Makes 24 pieces

Ingredients:

1/2 pound	smoked sockeye salmon, flaked
24 slices	baguette bread cut half inch thick
Caramelize:	
1/4 cup	olive oil
4 medium	Belgian endive cut into 1 inch slices
1 teaspoon	granulated sugar
1 teaspoon	salt
Dressing:	
1 large	lemon, juiced
1 medium	lime, juiced
2 tablespoons	olive oil
3 tablespoons	fresh dill, chopped
black pepper	to taste
Garnish:	several sprigs of fresh dill

To caramelize: In a large sauté pan, heat oil. Sauté Belgian endive slices, add sugar, and salt. Cook on high heat, stirring until endive is caramelized (endive turns light brown and resembles caramel color). Remove from heat and let stand.

Dressing: Mix all dressing ingredients together. Pour over salmon and let stand.

To Assemble: Place 1 teaspoon of salmon mixture on each slice of bread. Top with 1 teaspoon caramelized sliced Belgian endive in the center on top of the salmon mixture. Garnish with sprigs of fresh dill.

MINI SALMON CAKES

These salmon cakes can be done ahead of time. These mini cakes can be frozen before or after baking. They do not need to be defrosted to bake. Mini salmon cakes can be made in a large size and served for lunch or dinner, accompanied by a salad.

Prep time: 25 min. Cook time: 18 min. Makes approx. 45 pieces

Preheat oven to 400°

Ingredients:

1 pound	salmon fillet, cooked and shredded
1/4 cup	Panko bread crumbs
2 tablespoons	capers
2 teaspoons	Dijon mustard
3 teaspoons	Worcestershire sauce
1 medium	jalapeno, seeds and ribs removed, finely chopped
3 tablespoons	cilantro, chopped
2 medium	shallots, peeled and chopped
1 medium	red pepper, seeds and ribs removed, finely chopped
1 large	egg, beaten
2 tablespoons	crème fraîche
2 medium	limes, juiced and zested
4 tablespoons	olive oil for brushing

Combine salmon, Panko breadcrumbs, capers, mustard, Worcestershire sauce, jalapeno, cilantro, shallots, red pepper, beaten egg, crème fraîche, lime zest and juice. Shape into 1 inch round patties.

Oil a baking sheet, then brush each salmon cake with olive oil on both sides. Bake in oven for 10 minutes on one side then the other for 8 more minutes.

Serve with Aioli Sauce or Red Pepper Sauce (in Sauce section of cookbook).

BRIE - FALL BOUNTY

This Fall Bounty Brie is ideal for the Holiday season. This is an excellent appetizer to take as a hostess gift. It is easy to make. Other dried fruits and nuts of your choice may be substituted.

Prep time: 20 min. Serves 6-10

Ingredients:

1 (2.2 pound)	Brie wheel
8 ounces	cream cheese, softened
1/3 cup	dried cranberries or cherries
1/3 cup	dried apricots, chopped
1/3 cup	dried strawberries
1/3 cup	pistachio nuts
1/3 cup	dried mangos, chopped
1/3 cup	coconut, shredded
1/3 cup	hazelnuts, chopped

Open the Brie wheel. Remove from box. Unwrap the Brie without removing the wax paper on the bottom. Spread cream cheese on top and sides of Brie. Mark top of Brie into 7 equal portions and place each of the remaining ingredients on its 1/7th space. Make sure decorations extend down the sides. Remove Brie to a plate and discard paper.

INCREDIBLE MEATBALLS

These meatballs are great as an appetizer. Just serve as is or add to any of the sauces in the cookbook. This recipe is used in Tata's (Grandma's) chicken soup.

Prep time: 30 min. Cook time: 15 min. Makes 67 meatballs

Preheat oven to 350°

Ingredients:

2 pounds	chopped meat (1 pound beef or turkey and 1 pound pork or chicken)
1 large	onion, cut into 8^{ths}, finely chopped
1/2 bunch	parsley, stems removed, washed and dried
1 clove	garlic, peeled and crushed
1-1/2 slices	bread
1/2 cup	milk
1/2 teaspoon	allspice
1/2 teaspoon	nutmeg
2 teaspoons	salt
1 teaspoon	black pepper

Place meat in a large mixing bowl. Put onion, parsley and garlic in food processor bowl and process finely. Add to meat mixture.

Soak bread in milk, add allspice, nutmeg, salt and pepper. Add to meat mixture. Knead well. Form into little balls and place on a greased cookie sheet. Bake for 10-15 minutes until done. Remove and let cool.

SPINACH PHYLLO LOGS

These phyllo logs are great to freeze. Bake them the day of serving. Usually I keep at least one of them in the freezer. Great dish to take when invited to a potluck gathering.

Prep time: 35 min. Cook time: 35 min. Makes 3 logs

Preheat oven to 375°

Ingredients:

3/4 pound	butter, clarified
1 pound	package phyllo dough, defrosted

Filling:

20 ounces	frozen chopped spinach (drained and dried)
1 pound	ricotta cheese
1 pound	feta cheese, crumbled
1 bunch	fresh dill, chopped
1/2 teaspoon	white pepper
1 large	egg, beaten
1 teaspoon	salt

Clarify butter (see cooking terms). To defrost phyllo dough, leave at room temperature for at least 3 hours, or overnight in the refrigerator. Place the spinach in a bowl. Top with ricotta cheese, crumbled feta cheese, dill, pepper, beaten egg and salt. Mix them well.

Divide the filling and phyllo sheets into 3 equal parts. Cover all phyllo sheets with plastic wrap and top with moist towel. Work with one portion at a time. Remove the covering and brush each sheet of a portion of phyllo (approximately 8 sheets) with clarified butter. Add one third of filling 1-1/2 inch wide down the center of the length of the phyllo sheet. Roll phyllo sheet around stuffing (in a jelly roll manner) and brush with butter. Keep covered while doing the two other logs.

Wrap the logs with butcher paper or plastic wrap, chill until logs harden.

To prepare: Beginning from the center of the log, cut 1-inch slices from each side. Do not cut through the log. Each log makes approximately 15 slices. Place sliced log(s) on a buttered baking sheet. Bake for 30-35 minutes until golden brown. Unused portion of spinach phyllo logs should be wrapped well with plastic wrap then aluminum foil, sealed tightly and frozen. Frozen logs can be baked directly from the freezer. Increase baking time to 40 minutes.

Before serving Spinach Phyllo Log, cut pieces all the way through. Serve hot or at room temperature.

See photo on page 16

ORANGE SHRIMP

Leftover Orange Shrimp is great for lunch served with cooked rice. It also can be used to make a salad.

Prep time: 15 min. Cook time: 10 min. Makes 40 pieces

Ingredients:

40 large	shrimp, peeled and deveined
1/2 cup	olive oil or vegetable oil
3 inch piece	fresh ginger, peeled and sliced
1 bunch	green onions (scallions), trimmed and sliced
1 tablespoon	black pepper
2 medium	oranges, juiced and zested
1 teaspoon	cayenne pepper or dried, crushed red chili
salt to taste	

Steam shrimp until opaque in color. Mix all the remaining ingredients together. Add to steamed shrimp. Serve at room temperature. Use with toothpicks for easy serving.

SALADS

FARMER'S MARKET PASTA SALAD

This salad is great to take on a picnic or potluck gathering. I love making this salad after my visit to the Farmer's Market. Pistachio Walnut Vinaigrette dressing can be doubled, stored in the refrigerator for use on other salads. Tatsoi is a miniature oriental vegetable; it has dense rosettes of green leaves.

Prep time: 30 min. Cook time: 10 min. Serves 6

Ingredients:

1 pound	cooked campanelle, farfalle, or penne pasta
salt to taste	
2 tablespoons	olive oil
2 cups	arugula, washed, dried, stems removed and chopped
2 cups	mustard greens, chopped
2 cups	Tatsoi (Asian greens), or baby spinach, washed, dried and stems removed
1 cup	basil leaves, washed and chopped
2 medium	yellow zucchini, sliced
1 medium	Armenian cucumber, sliced
3 large	tomatoes, quartered

Pistachio Walnut Vinaigrette:

1/2 cup	raw pistachio nuts
1/2 cup	walnuts
1 teaspoon	Dijon mustard
1/4 cup	balsamic vinegar
3/4 cup	extra virgin olive oil
salt and pepper	to taste

Garnish:

2 tablespoons	pistachio nuts

Boil water in a large 6-quart pot. Add salt. When water has boiled, add pasta, stir gently. Boil uncovered 10 minutes for pasta al dente or follow package instructions. Drain pasta, place in a bowl and mix with olive oil. Set aside to cool.

Pistachio Walnut Vinaigrette Dressing: Meanwhile, in a blender or food processor, place all the pistachio walnut vinaigrette ingredients and puree until smooth.

Assembly: Place all greens on top of cooked pasta. Add remaining ingredients to cooked pasta. Mix together well.

To serve: Pour Pistachio Walnut Vinaigrette over pasta salad, mix well. Garnish with raw pistachio nuts.

SALADE NIÇOISE

Salade niçoise has lived on, pleasing generations of palates. At the beginning, it was a vegetable salad; anchovies and tuna later were added. Purists use anchovies, artichokes, and fava beans, especially in Provençe. If there is salad left over, make a sandwich called "pan bagnat", which literally means "wet bread". Cut baguettes in half, drizzle with vinegar, olive oil, salt and pepper. Place leftover salad between halves and press together firmly. Wrap well and refrigerate for at least an hour. Enjoy!

Prep time: 30 min. Cook time: 20 min. Serves 6

Ingredients:

3 large	hard cooked eggs, shelled and quartered
3 medium	Yukon potatoes, cooked and sliced
3 large	tomatoes, quartered
1/2 pound	tender fresh fava beans or string beans partially cooked
1 large	red pepper, seeded, ribs removed and sliced
1 large	green pepper, seeded, ribs removed and sliced
1-1/2 cups	marinated artichokes, drained
1 (2 ounce)	can anchovies fillets, drained (optional)
12 ounces	tuna, cooked or canned
1/4 cup	green olives
12 leaves	Boston lettuce washed and dried (optional)

Dressing:

2 cloves	garlic, peeled and crushed
2 tablespoons	red wine vinegar
2 tablespoons	freshly squeezed lemon juice
12 leaves	basil, chopped
1/2 cup	extra virgin olive oil
salt and pepper	to taste

Assembly: Arrange all ingredients separately on a large platter.

Dressing: In a small bowl, crush garlic, add salt and pepper. Whisk together wine vinegar and lemon juice. Add chopped basil, slowly add olive oil while whisking together.

To serve: Drizzle the dressing on the salad. Or place dressing in a container to dress each salad individually.

See photo on page 28

Salade Niçoise see recipe on page 27.

STUFFED BEET SALAD

Either yellow or red beets may be used in this recipe. Yellow beets are only available during the winter season and can be ordered at any produce store. This recipe is also great made with boiled potatoes instead of beets.

Prep time: 10 min. Cook time: 45 min. Serves 4

Ingredients:

4 medium	cooked beets, skinned
2 stalks	celery, peeled and finely chopped
1/4 cup	cooked peas
1/4 cup	mayonnaise
1 teaspoon	balsamic vinegar
salt and pepper	to taste
1 medium	Belgian endive

Beet Filling:

Cut off the top portion of beets, scoop inside with melon baller. Mix the scooped portion of beets with the chopped celery. Add peas, mayonnaise, vinegar, salt and pepper to taste. Fill the scooped beets with the beet filling. Place each beet on a Belgian endive leaf. Serve any extra filling on the side.

PANZANELLA - FATOUSH BREAD SALAD

This bread salad is quite popular in the Mediterranean region. The Tuscans call it Panzanella, the poor man's dinner. The Middle Eastern call it Fatoush. Fatoush is derived from the Middle Eastern's respect for bread—no bread is to be thrown away! As children when we accidentally dropped bread onto the floor, we were asked to pick it up and kiss it before feeding it to animals.

Prep time: 45 min. Serves 4-6

Ingredients:

Bread:

1/2 pound	Italian bread 3 to 4 days old, cut into 1 inch pieces or
2 loaves	pita bread, cut into 1 inch pieces
1 tablespoon	olive oil

Salad:

1 large	red onion, peeled and cut into 1/2 inch cubes
2 medium	cucumbers, peeled, seeded and cut into 1/2 inch cubes
5 medium	tomatoes, diced
1 cup	loosely packed fresh basil leaves, torn
1 cup	Italian parsley, washed dried and chopped
3 tablespoons	capers

Dressing:

1/4 cup	red wine vinegar or fresh lemon juice
2 cloves	garlic, peeled and crushed
1/2 cup	extra-virgin olive oil
salt and pepper	to taste

Topping:

3 ounces	shaved Parmesan cheese

Toss bread with olive oil and place under broiler until light brown.

Dressing: In a large mixing bowl, whisk together the vinegar or lemon juice, garlic and olive oil. Season with salt and pepper to taste.

Assembly: Mix all ingredients including the bread. Add dressing and toss to combine and let stand until the bread has absorbed some of the vinaigrette.

To serve: Top with shaved Parmesan cheese

CHICKEN SALAD WITH ORANGE PISTACHIO VINAIGRETTE DRESSING

This is an exotic salad to be served when entertaining. The combination of pears and the orange pistachio dressing are memorable. Parts of this salad can be prepared ahead of time: poach the chicken, blanch pea pods, cut peppers and make the Orange Pistachio Vinaigrette Dressing. Turkey or cooked shrimp may also be substituted for the chicken.

Prep time: 30 min. Cook time: 30 min. Serves 6

Ingredients:

Poaching Chicken:

1-1/2 pounds	chicken breast, skinless and boneless
2 cups	water
1 cup	white wine
4 leaves	basil
1 tablespoon	olive oil
salt and pepper	to taste

Salad Ingredients:

1/2 pound	pea pods, blanched, rinsed in cold water
1 medium	yellow or red pepper, seeded and sliced
3 medium	Belgian endive, washed, dried and leaves separated
1 medium	pear, sliced
1 small	radicchio, washed, dried, leaves separated and torn into bite size pieces

Orange Pistachio Vinaigrette:

1 medium	orange, zested and juiced
1 medium	shallot, peeled and cut in half
1/4 cup	raw pistachio nuts
1 tablespoon	Dijon mustard
1/4 cup	white wine vinegar
1/2 cup	extra virgin olive oil
white pepper	to taste
salt	to taste

To poach chicken: In a saucepan place water, wine, basil, olive oil, salt and pepper. Bring to a boil. Add chicken and simmer for 20 minutes until cooked. Remove chicken breasts, let cool. Cut chicken breasts into slices.

Orange Pistachio Vinaigrette Dressing: Place all ingredients for vinaigrette except oil in food processor bowl. Process until smooth. Pour in olive oil and process until well pureed.

To assemble salad: Place each salad ingredient in a separate self sealing plastic bag or bowl with some of the dressing and toss, then arrange on a serving plate.

See photo on page 32

Chicken Salad With Orange Pistachio Vinaigrette Dressing, *see recipe on page 31.*

SUMMER CORN SALAD

This salad may be prepared the day before serving. It is a favorite especially during the corn season. Frozen corn may be substituted when fresh corn is not available. Wonderful served as a salsa dip with corn chips. This whole salad could be prepared ahead allowing the flavors of all ingredients to blend together.

Prep time: 35 min. Cook time: 10 min. Serves 6

Ingredients:

8 ears	fresh corn, husked, blanched and kernels removed <u>or</u>
	4 cups frozen corn, defrosted
2 large	plums, pitted and diced
1/4 pound	baby carrots, blanched and horizontally sliced
1 medium	red onion, peeled and finely diced
1 large	yellow pepper, seeded, deveined and finely diced
1 large	red pepper, seeded, deveined and finely diced
1/2 bunch	cilantro, stems removed, washed, dried and chopped
1 bunch	green onions (scallions), trimmed and sliced
1 medium	mango, peeled, pitted and diced

Lime, Rice Vinegar Dressing:

3 medium	limes, juiced
1/2 cup	rice vinegar
1/2 cup	olive oil
salt and pepper	to taste

Lime, Rice Vinegar Dressing: Mix all dressing ingredients together and set aside.

Assembly: Place all salad ingredients in a large salad bowl. Add dressing and mix well.

SALATA HORIATIKI
COUNTRY GREEK SALAD

This is a typical Greek salad best served with pita bread. It tastes better if prepared an hour prior to serving.

Prep time: 30 min. Serves 8

Ingredients:

1 head	romaine lettuce, washed, dried and julienned
4 large	vine ripe tomatoes, cut into 8 wedges
2 medium	cucumbers, peeled and sliced
1 medium	red onion, thinly sliced
2 bunches	green onions, (scallions) trimmed and chopped
1 cup	pitted Kalamata olives
2 tablespoons	capers
1 (2 ounce)	can anchovies fillets (optional)
1 cup	feta cheese coarsely crumbled

Dressing:

4 tablespoons	red wine vinegar
2 tablespoons	fresh oregano leaves, chopped
1/2 teaspoon	salt
1 clove	garlic, peeled and crushed
1/3 cup	olive oil
ground pepper	to taste

Dressing: In a bowl, whisk vinegar, oregano, salt, crushed garlic, olive oil and pepper. Let stand.

Mix all ingredients except anchovies and feta. Toss with dressing an hour prior to serving.

To serve: Mix in feta and add anchovies if desired.

REFRESHER SALAD

The name refresher salad describes this salad. This salad is refreshing for hot summer days.

Prep time: 30 min. Serves 6

Ingredients:

2 large	pink grapefruits, peeled and sectioned
1 medium	red apple, unpeeled, cored and sliced into rings
1/4 cup	orange juice
1 medium	jicama, peeled, cut into matchsticks
1 medium	yellow pepper, seeded, deveined and sliced
1 medium	red pepper, seeded, deveined and sliced
15 large	radishes, stems removed and cut in half
1 medium	mango, peeled, pit removed and diced
3 medium	tomatillos, washed and sliced into rings

With a sharp knife, cut off and discard grapefruit peel and membrane. Over a bowl, cut between inner grapefruit membranes and lift out fruit segments. Place fruit segments in bowl and set aside. Save juice for the dressing mixture.

Dressing:

1/4 cup	orange juice
1/2 cup	grapefruit juice collected from membranes
1/4 cup	white wine vinegar
1/4 cup	cilantro leaves
1/4 teaspoon	salt
pepper	to taste

Dressing: Mix all dressing ingredients together except cilantro. Soak sliced apples in orange juice to prevent discoloring. Drain.

Toss vegetables and fruits with the dressing, drain and save dressing for later. Add cilantro to salad dressing and set aside. Assemble salad alternating vegetables and fruits in layers. Pour on remaining dressing and serve.

JARDINIÈRES SALMON SALAD

Jardinières in French means garden plants. This salad mixed with salmon and eggs is quite a satisfying meal. Most ingredients can be prepared ahead of time except for slicing the tomatoes and cucumbers just prior to assembling.

Prep time: 30 min. Cook time: 20 min. Serves 4-6

Ingredients:

1-1/2 pounds	cooked salmon, sliced
2 large	hard boiled eggs, shelled and sliced
3 medium	carrots, peeled, sliced and blanched
2 medium	yellow or red peppers, seeded and sliced
2 medium	vine ripe tomatoes, sliced
1/2 medium	English cucumber, sliced
1 small	red onion, peeled and sliced
1 cup	baby spinach, washed and dried
7 leaves	Frizee lettuce, washed, dried and torn into pieces *or* endive lettuce

Vinaigrette Dressing:

1 tablespoon	Dijon mustard
1 large	lemon, juiced
1/2 cup	balsamic vinegar
1 cup	olive oil
salt and pepper	to taste

Vinaigrette Dresssing: Place mustard, lemon juice, vinegar, salt and pepper into a food processor bowl and process. While processor is on, pour in oil and process several seconds. Set aside.

Poach, grill or bake salmon. Let cool, slice and set aside. Place each of the ingredients in a separate self sealing plastic bag and toss with some vinaigrette dressing.

Assembly: Use a glass salad bowl. Start by layering lettuce at the bottom. Add spinach, then continue layering until all vegetables have been used. Top with boiled eggs and salmon. Chill prior to serving.

AUTHENTIC TABBOULEH

Tabbouleh salad is one of my favorites. This recipe is an authentic Lebanese salad. It is best made in summer to take advantage of the ripe tomatoes. There are several variations for the tabbouleh depending on what part of the Middle East it originates. It is great as a side dish with grilled meat. This salad may be prepared ahead eliminating the salt. Prior to serving add salt and mix the salad.

Prep time: 30 min. Serves 6

Ingredients:

1/2 cup	cracked wheat or bulgur
4 bunches	Italian flat parsley, stems removed, washed, dried and chopped
4 medium	vine ripe tomatoes, diced
2 bunches	green onions (scallions), trimmed and sliced
1/2 teaspoon	allspice
1/2 cup	lemon juice
1/4 cup	olive oil
3 teaspoons	salt
white pepper	to taste
2 hearts	romaine lettuce, washed and separated into leaves

Rinse and drain cracked wheat. Squeeze out water. Using a food processor, chop parsley. Add parsley, tomatoes, green onions (scallions), allspice, lemon juice, olive oil, salt and pepper to cracked wheat. Toss together.

Serve with lettuce leaves.

"Julia Child" heirloom tomatoes

PAPA TAHINI SALAD

This salad was my Dad's favorite. It is great as a topping for the Imjadara- Lentil And Rice recipe. Making and eating this salad brought back many memories. This salad tastes better when prepared the day before. Prior to using Tahini, stir container thoroughly and refrigerate after opening.

Prep time: 20 min. Serves 4

Ingredients:

1 bunch	parsley, stems removed, washed and chopped
1/2 medium	red onion, peeled and chopped
2 large	tomatoes, diced
1 large	cucumber, peeled and diced
1 large	red pepper, diced
2 tablespoons	extra virgin olive oil

Tahini Dressing:

1/2 cup	Tahini
1/4 cup	water
1/2 cup	lemon juice
2 teaspoons	salt
1 teaspoon	pepper
2 tablespoons	balsamic vinegar

Tahini Dressing: Mix Tahini with water, lemon, salt, pepper and balsamic vinegar. Make sure it is smooth. If needed, use the food processor.

Assembly: Mix the dressing with the vegetables, drizzle the 2 tablespoons of extra virgin olive oil on top of salad.

LEAFY GREEN SALAD
BLUE CHEESE COGNAC DRESSING

This salad is great as an accompaniment with pork or lamb. The Blue Cheese Cognac dressing makes this salad exotic. Recommend this salad after a meal. The dressing is wonderful when used on fruits as a fruit salad.

Prep time: 15 min. Serves 4

Ingredients:

4 leaves	butter lettuce, washed, dried and cut into bite sizes
4 leaves	endive lettuce, washed, dried and cut into bite sizes
3 leaves	spinach, washed, dried and cut into bite sizes
2 leaves	romaine, washed, dried and cut into bite sizes

Blue Cheese Cognac Dressing:

6 ounces	blue cheese, crumbled
1/3 cup	walnuts, broken into chunks
2 tablespoons	cognac
4 tablespoons	walnut oil
2 tablespoons	cider vinegar

Dressing: Place all the dressing ingredients in a food processor and process until smooth.

Assembly: Arrange lettuce greens in salad bowl, and toss with dressing just prior to serving.

APPLE FIELD GREEN SALAD

Either apples or pears may be used in this recipe. This salad may be served before or after a meal.

Prep time: 20 min. Serves 4

Ingredients:

2 medium	apples (Jonathan, Gala, Empire or Red Delicious), sliced
1/2 cup	apple juice or orange juice to soak apples
6 cups	mixed greens, washed and dried
2 medium	Belgian endive, washed and leaves separated
1/4 cup	large macadamia nuts, whole
4 ounces	Gorgonzola cheese, crumbled

Apple Vinaigrette Dressing:

1/4 cup	apple juice
3 tablespoons	apple vinegar
3 tablespoons	olive oil
salt to taste	

Soak apple slices in 1/2 cup orange juice until ready to use.

Apple Vinaigrette Dressing: Make dressing by mixing all dressing ingredients in a bowl.

Place field greens on a platter. Remove apples from juice, reserving 1/4 cup for dressing.

Assembly: Arrange apples in a spoke fashion and endive leaves in a circle.

Pour dressing on top. Place nuts in center of salad. Crumble cheese on top.

ORZO CANNELLINI SALAD

This salad is better if done a couple of hours before serving so flavors can be infused together. Serve with a nice crusty bread. A must to make in July and August when tomatoes are in abundance. The lemon dressing is a personal favorite.

Prep time: 20 min. Cook time: 15 min. Serves 4

Ingredients:

1 cup	uncooked orzo
1 tablespoon	olive oil
2 (15 ounce)	cans cannellini beans, drained
3 large	vine ripe tomatoes, diced
1 large	English cucumber, diced
1 bunch	green onions (scallions), sliced
2 tablespoons	fresh tarragon leaves, chopped
2 tablespoons	fresh oregano leaves, chopped
Lemon Dressing:	
3 cloves	garlic, peeled and crushed
1 large	lemon, juiced
1/2 cup	extra virgin olive oil
salt and pepper	to taste

Lemon Dressing: Mix all dressing ingredients together. Set aside.

Cook orzo according to package pasta instructions, preferably al dente. Drain and mix with olive oil.

Assembly: Place all remaining ingredients in a large salad bowl and toss salad with dressing.

SOUPS

BEEF STOCK

Stocks are great to make and freeze. Store in the freezer in 2-cup containers. Stocks can be used for soups, stews, sauces, rice and it can be used to sauté and poach meats, fish and vegetables.

Prep time: 20 min. Cook time: 2 - 3 hrs. Makes 5 quarts

Preheat oven to 450°

Ingredients:

3 - 4 pounds	beef bones, washed and fat removed
2 each	carrots, celery stalks, tomatoes, garlic cloves and onions
3 tablespoons	Worcestershire sauce
salt and pepper	to taste
Bouquet Garni	see recipe
6 quarts	water

Peel and cut carrots, onions and garlic into chunks. Cut celery and tomatoes. Place all vegetables and bones in a roasting pan. Add Worcestershire sauce and season with salt and pepper.

Bake in the upper third of oven until brown. Remove fat. Remove bones and vegetables and place in a stockpot. Add water and Bouquet Garni.

Deglaze roasting pan with water and add to the stockpot. Simmer for 2 hours. Keep skimming scum as it rises. The longer the beef stock cooks the better it tastes. If water evaporates, add a little boiling water.

When stock is ready, strain with a colander lined with cheesecloth into another pot. Can be stored in containers in the refrigerator or freezer.

BOUQUET GARNI

Make several Bouquet Garni and store them in the freezer for future use. It can also be purchased in gourmet stores.

Makes one bundle

Ingredients:

2 medium	bay leaves
12 sprigs	fresh parsley
6 sprigs	fresh thyme
12 whole	peppercorns
6 sprigs	basil
6 sprigs	tarragon

Cut a 3x3 inch square piece of cheesecloth. Place all of the above ingredients into the center of the cloth and tie into a bundle with a string.

CHICKEN STOCK

Stocks are great to make and freeze. Store in the freezer in 2- cup containers. Stocks can be used for soups, stews, sauces and rice. It can be used to sauté and poach meats, fish and vegetables. The cooked chicken that was used for the stock can be used for Tata's Soup. Also it can be shredded and used in the Chicken Salad with Orange Pistachio Vinaigrette.

Prep time: 20 min. Cook time: 2 hrs. 45 min. Makes 5 quarts

Ingredients:

1 (4 - 5 pound)	whole chicken
7 quarts	water
1 medium	onion, peeled and cut into 1/8ths
4 medium	carrots, peeled and sliced
4 stalks	celery, sliced
5 cloves	garlic, peeled
1 stick	cinnamon
1 teaspoon	allspice
4 teaspoons	salt
2 teaspoons	pepper
1 Bouquet Garni	See recipe

Wash, clean and remove fat and giblets from chicken. Put chicken and 7 quarts of water in a large stockpot. Add onion, carrots, celery, garlic, cinnamon, allspice, salt, pepper and Bouquet Garni.

Cover and bring to a rapid boil, then simmer on medium heat for at least 2 hours and 45 minutes until chicken is well cooked and falls apart. Let cool, drain and reserve liquid broth. Remove bones and skin from chicken.

Borscht Soup in Martini Glass, see recipe on page 45.

BORSCHT

Borscht can be served cold as well as warm. It is a soup of Russian origin. A very old Russian friend introduced me to this soup. When served cold use martini glasses and garnish with sour cream and dill.

Prep time: 35 min. Cook time: 1 hr. Serves 10

Ingredients:

3-1/2 quarts	beef broth
5 medium	fresh beets, peeled and diced into 1/2 inch pieces <u>or</u> two 15 ounce cans of whole beets, reserving 1 cup of juice
2 medium	carrots, peeled and diced into 1/2 inch pieces
2 medium	potatoes, peeled and diced into 1/2 inch pieces
1 medium	onion, peeled and diced into 1/2 inch pieces
1 medium	parsnip, peeled and diced into 1/2 inch pieces
1/2 head	cabbage, thinly sliced
1/2 cup	red wine vinegar
salt and pepper	to taste

Optional Ingredients:

1 pound	top sirloin, diced
2 tablespoons	olive oil

Topping:

16 ounces	sour cream
1/3 cup	chopped dill

Place broth in a large stockpot (approximately 8 quarts). Add all diced vegetables. If using canned beets add them at the end, along with the 1 cup of reserved beet juice. Add sliced cabbage and bring soup to a boil. Lower heat and simmer for 55 minutes. Add 1/2 cup red wine vinegar. Simmer on low heat for 5 minutes.

Optional:
Dice meat into 1/2 inch cubes. Sauté in olive oil, salt and pepper and hold until serving.

To Serve:
Place some Borscht in serving bowl, then add meat. Top with 1 tablespoon of sour cream and sprinkle with chopped dill.

SAFFRON VEGETABLE SOUP

Saffron also known as safran. The saffron plant is of Eastern origin and introduced into Spain by the Arabs. It is also cultivated in France. Saffron contains a volatile oil and a coloring substance, which enhances the flavor and appearance of this soup.

Prep time: 30 min. Cook time: 1 hr. Serves 6-8

Ingredients:

2 medium	green zucchini, diced
1 medium	sweet potato, peeled and diced
1 large	eggplant, partially peeled and diced
1 medium	red onion, peeled and diced
2 medium	carrots, peeled and diced
2 medium	yellow zucchini, peeled and diced
1 large	tomato, diced
6 small	mushrooms, sliced
6 cloves	garlic, peeled, sliced or whole
1/2 pound	pea pods
5 sprigs	fresh basil leaves, chopped
2 tablespoons	olive oil
3 quarts (12 cups)	water, vegetable or chicken broth
salt and pepper	to taste
1 pinch	saffron
1 cup	orzo
Bouquet Garni	see recipe
8 slices	toasted garlic bread topped with chèvre or Swiss cheese

Heat olive oil in a large sauté pan. Sauté onion and garlic, add all vegetables a little at a time until coated in oil. Remove and place in the stockpot filled with water or broth. Add basil and Bouquet Garni to soup. Bring to a boil. Add salt, pepper and saffron. Simmer for 45 minutes. Add orzo and cook another 15 minutes on simmer. Remove Bouquet Garni before serving.

To serve: Place in soup bowl, top with garlic toast.

DRIED FRUIT SOUP

A cup of warm dried fruit soup will cheer the coldest winter day. Try it for breakfast or dessert. Serve cold or warm and top with chopped nuts and a dash of ground cinnamon. A fabulous source of fiber. This soup originated in the Middle East. It is usually served to guests when a baby is born.

Prep time: 10 min. Cook time: 1hr. 30 min. Serves 10

Ingredients:

1 cup	barley, or whole wheat grain
4 cups	boiling water
1/2 cup	sugar
15 dried	prunes
15 dried	apricots
2 cups	golden raisins
1 stick	cinnamon
2 tablespoons	rose water or vanilla extract
1 (46 ounce)	can apricot nectar
2 tablespoons	crushed anise

Garnish:

1 cup	chopped nuts, pistachios, walnuts or almonds
1 tablespoon	ground cinnamon

Soak barley or wheat in water overnight. Drain. Cover with 4 cups of boiling water and simmer until tender. Add more water as needed. Barley should be tender after 1 hour.

Add to barley the sugar, dried fruits, cinnamon sticks, rose water or vanilla, apricot nectar and anise. Simmer for 20-30 minutes.

Pour into teacups or small bowls and garnish with chopped nuts and ground cinnamon.

TATA'S (GRANDMA'S) CHICKEN SOUP

This soup is very festive when served as a main course. My Tata used to make this soup on someone's birthday, Christmas Eve or when someone had a baby. This was served during special celebrations. It was also very comforting when we were sick. The chicken stock and meatballs can be made ahead of time and frozen. Frozen meatballs can be added to the broth.

Prep time: 20 min. Cook time: 30 min. Serves 8-10

Ingredients:

6 quarts	chicken stock or 24 cups of chicken broth
1/2 cup	orzo or long grain rice
5 cups	cooked chicken, boned and shredded
1-1/2 pounds	cooked meatballs (see recipe for meatballs)
1/2 bunch	parsley, stems removed, washed and chopped
1 large	lemon, juiced

Place 6 quarts of chicken stock in a large soup pot. Add orzo or rice. Cook together for 10 minutes. Add cooked chicken then add the cooked meatballs. Just before serving, add parsley and lemon juice.

LENTIL SOUP WITH SPINACH-CARROTS

This is a nutritional, healthy soup. It is great to eat the next day as a cold side dish accompanied with a meat, fish or poultry. Alone this is a wonderful soup for your vegetarian friends.

Prep time: 15 min. Cook time: 40 min. Serves 8

Ingredients:

1/4 cup	olive oil
1 medium	onion, peeled and chopped
4 cloves	garlic, peeled and crushed
salt and pepper	to taste
1 teaspoon	cumin
2 cups	dry lentils, washed and drained
8 cups	water
4 medium	carrots, peeled and sliced
1 pound	fresh spinach leaves, washed
8 ounces	fettuccine noodles
1/4 cup	balsamic vinegar

Topping

1 whole	pita bread, opened in half
1 clove	garlic, crushed
2 tablespoons	olive oil

In a 4-quart stockpot, heat oil until bubbly. Add onion, crushed garlic, salt and pepper to taste. Add cumin, lentils and 8 cups water to the stockpot. Cover, bring to a boil and cook on high heat for 20 minutes. Uncover, add carrots, spinach and fettuccine. Cover and simmer for approximately 20 minutes or until all vegetables and pasta are cooked. Remove from heat and add balsamic vinegar prior to serving.

Spread pita with garlic, oil, and cut into triangles to use as garnish for the soup.

LAMB SHANK SOUP
WITH WHITE BEANS & SPINACH

Lamb and beans happen to be my favorite two ingredients. This soup, served with a crusty loaf of French bread, is incredibly satisfying. Serve it for dinner or lunch, with an accompaniment of salad.

Prep time: 35 min. Cook time: 1 hr. 45 min. Serves 6

Ingredients:

4 medium	lamb shanks, fat removed
salt and pepper	to taste
1 teaspoon	allspice
1 pound	white dried beans, soaked overnight
6 quarts	water
1 head	garlic, peeled and separated into cloves
2 medium	onions, peeled and chopped
1 teaspoon	cumin
2 bunches	spinach, washed, stems removed and chopped (or two (10 ounce) frozen packages)
1 cup	vermicelli noodles

Wash lamb shanks and place in stockpot. Cover with water at least 1 inch above meat. Add salt, pepper and allspice. Bring to a boil then reduce heat to simmer for 30 minutes. Skim off fat.

Drain soaked beans and place in a large stockpot. Add the 6 quarts water, garlic, onions and cumin. Cook for approximately 1 hour.

Mix lamb shanks, lamb shank broth, beans and bean broth. Add spinach and vermicelli. Simmer for 15 minutes until vermicelli is thoroughly cooked.

SOUPE A L'OIGNON
ONION SOUP

This onion soup is delicious as a meal. There is nothing better than a hot Soupe A L'oignon on a cold winter day. It reminds me of Les Halles in Paris where they serve the best onion soup, especially at 2 in the morning! This onion soup freezes well.

Prep time: 20 min. Cook time: 2 hrs. Serves 10

Ingredients:

5 quarts (20 cups)	beef stock or broth
10 large	onions, peeled and sliced
2 ounces	butter
1/4 cup	olive oil
salt and pepper	to taste
3 teaspoons	sugar
3 cups	port wine
4 tablespoons	cognac
10 slices	toasted French bread
10 slices	Swiss or Gruyère cheese

Depending on the size of the sauté pan used, divide onions, butter and oil into approximately equal amounts. Sauté onions in a little olive oil and butter. Sprinkle with some of the sugar, salt and pepper and cook on medium to high heat until onions are quite brown in color. Repeat until all onions are done.

Deglaze the sauté pan by adding some broth. Place beef stock in a large stockpot. Add cooked onions. Cover and bring to a boil. Simmer for 40 minutes. Add port wine and cognac; cook over low heat for another 20 minutes.

Pour soup into an ovenproof dish and top with slices of toasted bread and cheese. Or serve by placing soup in individual ovenproof dishes and top with bread and cheese. Broil until bubbly.

Soupe A L'Oignon – Onion Soup, see recipe on page 51.

PASTAS

SPAGHETTINI WITH CLAMS AND MUSSELS IN MARINARA SAUCE

Show off your culinary talents without fussing! This dish is a very impressive meal to serve when entertaining guests.

Prep time: 30 min. Cook time: 15–20 min. Serves 4

Cook time does not include Marinara Sauce

Ingredients:

4 cups	Marinara Sauce
1 pound	fresh littleneck clams
1 pound	fresh mussels
1 cup	cornstarch
1 cup	Parmesan Reggiano cheese, freshly grated

Spaghettini:

1/2 pound	spaghettini
6-8 quarts	water
2 tablespoons	salt
1/2 medium	raw potato

Clean clams and mussels by scrubbing them with a brush. Place them in a bowl and cover with water. Add 1 cup cornstarch. Remove clams and mussels without disturbing bottom of water. If necessary, repeat process until no residue of sand is visible. Rinse clams and mussels several times to assure all the sand has been removed.

In a 6-8 quart pot, bring the Marinara Sauce to a simmer. Add clams and mussels. Cover and cook on medium until the clams and mussels begin opening their shells. Discard unopened ones.

Cooking Pasta: Fill a large pasta pot with 6-8 quarts water. Add salt and 1/2 raw potato. Bring to a rapid boil. Add spaghettini and stir with a fork. Bring again to another rapid boil, lower heat and simmer for at least 10-15 minutes or follow package directions. Pasta should be al dente. Drain and remove potato. Place in serving bowls and toss with desired amount of sauce.

To serve: Top with freshly grated Parmesan Reggianno cheese (optional).

See photo on page 56

PUTTANESCA SAUCE WITH FARFALLE PASTA

In Italy, this sauce got its name after an Italian lady of ill repute who wanted to entertain guests. She found all the ingredients for this sauce in her pantry and Voila! Puttanesca sauce is a lifesaver when done ahead and frozen. Just heat the sauce and cook pasta. Unused pasta sauces can be refrigerated or frozen.

Prep time: 10 min. Cook time: 30-40 min. Serves 8

Ingredients:

2 tablespoons	extra virgin olive oil
1 (2 ounce)	can of anchovies, drained chopped
4 cloves	garlic, peeled and crushed
4 cups	crushed tomatoes or Marinara Sauce
1 (7 ounce)	jar capers, drained
1 cup	black olives, pitted and chopped
1 cup	pitted green olives
3/4 cup	fresh basil leaves, chopped
1/2 teaspoon	red pepper flakes
1 cup	fresh grated Parmesan Reggiano or crumbled Feta cheese

Farfalle Pasta:

1 pound	farfalle pasta
6-8 quarts	water
3 tablespoons	salt
1/2 medium	raw potato

In a large 6-8 quart pot, heat the olive oil over medium heat. Add the drained anchovies and crushed garlic. Stir with back of spoon to mash anchovies. Add the crushed tomatoes or marinara sauce and bring to a simmer. Stir in the capers, olives, basil and red pepper flakes. Cook for 30 minutes on low heat stirring occasionally.

Cooking pasta: In a large pasta pot, add at least 6 quarts of water, salt, and raw potato. Bring to a rapid boil. Lower heat and cook according to package directions for approximately 10-15 minutes until pasta is al dente. Drain, discard potato. Toss pasta with desired amount of sauce and top with freshly grated Parmesan Reggiano or crumbled Feta cheese.

See photo on page 56

Spaghettini With Clams And Mussels in Marinara Sauce, see recipe on page 54.

Puttanesca Sauce with Farfalle Pasta, see recipe on page 55.

Tagliate Pasta With Garbanzo Beans – Pasta E Ceci, see recipe on page 58.

Campanelle Pasta Cassserole With Gorgonzola Sauce, see recipe on page 59.

TAGLIATE PASTA WITH GARBANZO BEANS
PASTA E CECI

This dish is famous in the region of Naples and eaten mostly in winter. However, I love this dish any time of the year. It is a party dish. The Pasta E Ceci takes no time to make. Stock pasta, garbanzo beans and broth in the pantry and viola, 15 minutes later a meal is cooked. While making the sauce, cook the pasta.

Prep time: 10 min. Cook time: 15 min. Serves 8

Ingredients:

Ceci Sauce (makes 4 cups)

2 tablespoons	olive oil
4 cloves	garlic, peeled and crushed
2 (14 ounce)	cans of garbanzo beans, drained
1-1/2 cups	chicken broth
1 teaspoon	cumin
1 bunch	cilantro, stems removed, washed, dried and chopped
1/2 cup	feta cheese, crumbled
salt and pepper	to taste
1 pound	fettuccini tagliate or spaghettini
6-8 quarts	water
3 tablespoons	salt
1/2 medium	raw potato

Ceci Sauce: In a large sauté pan, heat olive oil, crushed garlic cloves, and drained garbanzo beans. Cook together, add broth and cumin. Simmer covered for 15 minutes. Add chopped cilantro and crumbled feta cheese. Add salt and pepper to taste. Stir and set aside.

Cooking pasta: In a large pasta pot, add at least 6 quarts of water, salt and potato. Bring to a rapid boil. Add pasta and stir with a fork. Bring the water to a rapid boil again. Lower heat and cook for 10 minutes until al dente. Drain, remove potato. Place pasta in Ceci Sauce in a sauté pan, cook over medium heat for 2 minutes.

To serve: Remove from heat and serve in individual pasta bowls.

See photo on page 57

CAMPANELLE PASTA CASSEROLE WITH GORGONZOLA SAUCE

Great recipe can be assembled ahead of time. Refrigerate or freeze. Bake same day prior to serving. Panko can be purchased in most supermarkets. This definitely is a crowd pleaser.

Prep time: 10 min. Cook time: 25 min. Serves 8 - 10

Ingredients:

1 pound	campanelle pasta
6-8 quarts	water
3 tablespoons	salt
1/2 medium	raw potato

Gorgonzola Sauce:

1 cup	plain, low-fat or goat yogurt
2 tablespoons	dry sherry
1-1/2 cups	Gorgonzola cheese, crumbled (1/4 cup reserved)
freshly grated	black pepper to taste
1/2 cup	Panko bread crumbs
1/2 cup	pistachio nuts, chopped

Cooking pasta: Fill a large 6-8 quart pot with water, add salt and a raw potato. Bring to a rapid boil. Add the campanelle pasta. Stir with a fork. Bring to a boil again. Lower heat. Cook until just tender, al dente, following package directions.

Meanwhile combine the yogurt, sherry, and 1-1/4 cups of crumbled Gorgonzola cheese in a medium saucepan and whisk constantly over low heat until cheese melts in about 5 minutes. Drain the pasta when done, remove potato. Return the pasta to the pot and add the Gorgonzola sauce. Stir over medium low heat until the sauce thickens slightly, about 2 minutes. Add pepper to taste. Pour the mixture into a 3-quart 9x13x2 inch oven proof baking dish. Sprinkle Panko bread crumbs and chopped pistachios on top of the pasta mixture and dot with the remaining 2 ounces of Gorgonzola cheese. Brown the casserole under the broiler very close to the flames for about 5 minutes.

The recipe can be assembled ahead of time. Heat covered in the oven for 10 minutes, then uncover and broil for 5 minutes, or until light brown.

See photo on page 57

Pasta Provençal, see recipe on page 62.

Fettuccini With Wild Mushroom Creamy Sauce, see recipe on page 63.

PASTA PROVENÇAL

Pasta Provençal a very popular dish in Provençe, South of France. The use of the orange zest is typical of the region. Also a fabulous dish for a hot summer day. Can be eaten at room temperature. Great do ahead for buffet and al Fresco entertaining.

Prep time: 15 min. Cook time: 37 min. for sauce and pasta Serves 6

Ingredients:

1 medium	red onion, peeled and sliced
1 medium	fennel bulb, trimmed and cut into matchsticks
6 tablespoons	extra virgin olive oil
4 cloves	garlic, peeled and crushed
1/8 teaspoon	dried, crushed red chilies
1 dried	bay leaf
1 teaspoon	Herbes de Provençe
salt to taste	
1 (28 ounce)	can diced tomatoes with juice
1 medium	orange, zested
3/4 cup	Niçoise black olives, pitted
1 pound	dried pasta of your choice
1/2 cup	pine nuts, roasted
1/4 cup	Italian parsley, washed, dried, stems removed and chopped
6 teaspoons	chèvre (goat cheese)

In a large Dutch oven, heat olive oil. Sauté onion, fennel, add garlic, crushed red chilies, bay leaf, Herbes de Provençe and salt. Cook for 10 minutes. Add the diced tomatoes with the juice and zest of an orange. Add olives to sauce. Simmer until sauce begins to thicken, approximately 15 minutes. Remove and let rest. Taste for seasoning.

Cooking pasta: In a large pot bring 6 quarts of water to a rolling boil. Add 3 tablespoons salt. Add pasta, stirring to prevent sticking. Cook for about 12 minutes until pasta is al dente. Drain and add pasta to sauce, toss, turn heat to low and let rest for 1 to 2 minutes, stirring to coat pasta with sauce.

To serve: Place Pasta Provençal in a large serving pasta bowl, add chopped parsley and pine nuts toss together. Top with chèvre cheese.

See photo on page 60

FETTUCCINI WITH WILD MUSHROOM CREAMY SAUCE

This dish is an easy and delicious dish to make for entertaining. The creamy white sauce can be made ahead and refrigerated. Mushrooms can be cooked the day before. While boiling pasta, you can combine sauce with mushrooms and heat together.

Prep time: 20 min. Cook time: 22 min. Serves 8

Creamy Sauce:

10 ounces	chèvre, goat cheese
1 cup	cream, milk, half & half or low-fat milk
1 cup	chicken broth
1 cup	feta cheese, crumbled
1 teaspoon	nutmeg

Mushroom Mixture:

8 ounces	crimini mushrooms, sliced (Golden Italian)
8 ounces	portabella mushrooms, sliced
8 ounces	white mushrooms, sliced
1 tablespoon	olive oil
4 cloves	garlic, peeled and crushed
4 sprigs	sage leaves, chopped
salt and pepper	to taste
1 tablespoon	cognac
1/2 bunch	basil leaves, chopped
1 pound	fettuccini pasta
1 cup	Asiago cheese, grated
6-8 quarts	water
3 tablespoons	salt
1/2 medium	raw potato

Creamy Sauce: In a food processor or a blender, place all creamy sauce ingredients. Process together until a creamy texture. Set aside.

Clean mushrooms with a wet towel or wash, dry and slice. Place 1 tablespoon olive oil in large sauté pan. Cook mushrooms. Add crushed garlic, sage, salt and pepper to taste. Simmer on low heat until mushrooms are tender. Add cognac and simmer for 5 minutes.

Combine creamy sauce with mushroom mixture. Heat together for a few minutes. Turn off heat and add basil.

Cooking pasta: Cook pasta by filling a 6-8 quart pot with water. Add salt and potato. Bring to a rapid boil. Add fettuccini and stir with a fork. Bring to another boil. Lower heat to medium and cook according to package directions or 10-15 minutes until pasta is al dente. Drain, remove potato and discard.

To serve: Toss pasta with desired portion of mushroom sauce. Top with grated Asiago cheese.

See photo on page 61

Peppers and Eggplants

PAËLLA, RICE, RISOTTO

PAËLLA ALLA VALENCIANA
SEAFOOD PAËLLA

This recipe is from a Spanish friend from Valencia. Paëlla alla Valenciana specializes in combining seafoods and vegetables. It is fabulous; however, it tends to be pricey to prepare. It is a festive and colorful dish. I usually do this dish for special people. The name Paëlla comes from the iron frying pan with two handles, in which the rice is cooked and served.

Prep time: 1 hr. Cook time: 1 hr. Serves 8-10

Preheat oven to 375°

Ingredients:

1/4 cup	olive oil
1 large	red onion, peeled and diced
4 cloves	garlic, peeled and crushed
4 large	tomatoes, chopped
2 large	red peppers, seeded and sliced
2 large	yellow peppers, seeded and sliced
1/2 bunch	fresh Italian parsley, stems removed, washed, dried and chopped
2 cups	artichoke hearts, drained and cut in half
2 cups	frozen peas, defrosted
Seafood Mixture:	
10 large	clams, cleaned and steamed
10 large	mussels, cleaned and steamed
4 tablespoons	olive oil
1 pound	squid, cleaned and sliced
1 pound	shrimp, deveined
1 pound	scallops
Rice:	
2 cups	long grain rice
4 cups	chicken broth
1/2 teaspoon	saffron
salt and pepper	to taste
2 cups	pitted black olives
2 large	limes, juiced

In a large sauté pan or a 3-quart paëlla pan with cover, heat olive oil, sauté onion, garlic, tomatoes and peppers. Cook together until vegetables are softened, not over cooked. Add chopped parsley, artichoke hearts, peas and set aside.

Steam clams and mussels until shells open. If some shells stay closed, discard. In the same 3-quart Paëlla pan, heat olive oil, sauté squid, shrimp and scallops. Add the sautéed vegetables to the seafood mixture except the clams and mussels. Stir together. Heat broth in a saucepan, add saffron and let steep for 5 minutes. Add steeped saffron, broth, rice, salt and pepper to Paëlla. Cover and bring to boil on medium high heat. Place in oven to bake for 15 minutes. Add black olives, steamed clams and mussels. Cover and continue baking for another 15 minutes until rice is cooked. Remove from oven and let stand for 5 minutes. Pour lime juice on top and serve.

See photo on page 69

RISOTTO FINOCCHI
RISOTTO WITH FENNEL

This is an amazing comfort dish to enjoy. This accompaniment risotto is great with grilled chicken, fish or meat. It is a treat to share this Risotto Finocchi with family and friends.

Prep time: 15 min. Cook time: 37 min. Serves 6

Ingredients:

4 tablespoons	butter
2 tablespoons	olive oil
1 large	fennel with leaves, washed and sliced
1-1/2 cup	Arborio rice
6 cups	boiling vegetable, beef or chicken broth
salt and pepper	to taste
3/4 cup	Parmesan Reggiano, cheese grated

Melt 2 tablespoons butter and 2 tablespoons olive oil in a 2-quart pan. Sauté sliced fennel until it begins to soften. Add rice and sauté until well coated. Slowly pour in boiling broth. Add salt and pepper if needed to boiling broth. Cook rice over moderate heat, continue stirring and adding the boiling broth until it has been absorbed and the rice has become tender. Remove from heat.

Stir in the remaining 2 tablespoons of butter and the Parmesan Reggiano cheese. Cover by wrapping a towel over the lid. Keep risotto covered with a wrapped towel for 5 more minutes.

See photo on page 68

Risotto Finocchi – Risotto with Fennel, see recipe on page 68.

Paëlla Alla Valenciana – Seafood Paëlla, see recipe on page 66.

CHICKEN SAUSAGE PAËLLA

Paëlla is a Spanish rice dish. Different regions of Spain vary the paëlla according to local produce. Vegetable, meat, chicken and sausage characterize the paëlla of interior Spain. This recipe is great when all the vegetables are cut and cooked ahead of time. The vegetable mixture could be frozen and defrosted the day of making the Paëlla. When preparing this recipe, I make an extra batch and freeze it. The day of cooking the Paëlla, I just add rice, meats or fish.

Prep time: 1 hr. Cook time: 1 hr. Serves 8-10

Preheat oven to 375°

Ingredients:

1/4 cup	olive oil
1 large	red onion, peeled and diced
4 cloves	garlic, peeled and crushed
4 large	tomatoes, chopped
2 medium	red peppers, seeded and sliced
2 medium	yellow peppers, seeded and sliced
1/2 bunch	fresh Italian parsley, stems removed, washed, dried and chopped
2 cups	artichoke hearts, drained and cut in half
2 cups	frozen peas, defrosted

Chicken – Sausage Mixture:

4 tablespoons	olive oil
1 pound	chicken breast, sliced and diced into 1/2 inch pieces
1 pound	veal, chicken or Portuguese (Linguisa) sausage, sliced into 1 inch pieces
1 pound	Italian sausage, sliced into 1 inch pieces

Rice:

2 cups	long grain rice
4 cups	chicken broth
1/2 teaspoon	saffron
salt and pepper	to taste
2 cups	pitted black olives
2 large	limes, juiced

In a large sauté pan or 3-quart paëlla pan with cover, heat olive oil, sauté onion, garlic, tomatoes and peppers. Cook together until vegetables are softened, not overcooked. Add chopped parsley, artichoke hearts, peas and set aside.

Heat olive oil in the same paëlla pan. Sauté chicken, remove with slotted spoon and set aside. Sauté sausages, set aside. Place vegetable mixture in the pot where chicken and sausage were sautéed. Add chicken -sausage mixture to vegetables. Stir together. Heat broth in a saucepan, add saffron and let steep for 5 minutes. Add saffron broth, rice, salt and pepper to paëlla. Cover and bring to boil on medium high heat. Place in oven to bake for 15 minutes. Add black olives, cover and continue baking for another 15 minutes until rice is cooked. Remove from oven and let stand for 5 minutes. Pour lime juice on top and serve.

IMJADARA RICE AND LENTILS

Great recipe for lunch when unexpected company arrives. Also it is a lifesaver when you forget to defrost meat. Suggest keeping lentils and rice as a staple in your pantry. This dish is delicious when eaten at room temperature on a hot summer day.

Prep time: 10 min. Cook time: 25 min. Serves 8

Ingredients:

2 tablespoons	olive oil
1 large	red onion, peeled and chopped
4 cloves	garlic, peeled and crushed
2 cups	lentils, washed
2 teaspoons	cumin
salt and pepper	to taste
6 cups	water
1 cup	long grain rice, brown rice or bulgur

Topping:

1/4 cup	olive oil
4 large	onions, peeled and sliced.

In a 16-cup (2 quart) pot, heat oil, sauté onion and garlic. Add lentils, cumin, salt and pepper, then water. Bring to boil, simmer 15 minutes or until lentils are tender. Add rice and simmer covered for 15 to 20 minutes until rice is done.

Sauté onions in olive oil until caramelized.

To Serve: Place Imjadara on serving platter and top with caramelized onions.

A good accompaniment for the Imjadara is Papa Tahini Salad.

Peach Orchards

Nectarines

FONDUTAS, BAGNAS, DIPS

FETA - CHÈVRE FONDUTA

This is a very tasty fondue. The combination of both cheeses is very appetizing. The addition of the potato buds thickens the fondue. Wooden skewers are recommended for sanitary reasons.

Prep time: 10 min. Serves 6-8

Ingredients:

2 teaspoons	olive oil
1 tablespoon	potato buds, cornstarch or flour for thickening
3/4 cup	low-fat milk, broth or half and half
1 clove	fresh garlic, peeled and crushed
4 tablespoons	feta cheese, crumbled or cut into pieces
8 ounces	chèvre, crumbled
dash	Tabasco sauce

For dipping:

1 baguette	French bread, cut into bite sizes
1 basket	cherry tomatoes
1 large	cucumber, cubed into bite sizes

In a 2-quart fondue pot, heat olive oil over low heat. Add potato buds, cornstarch, or flour. Stir together. Mix in milk and heat. Add crushed garlic. Remove from heat. Add crumbled feta and chèvre cheese. Stir constantly in a figure eight pattern until cheese has melted. Add Tabasco sauce.

Place in a fondue pot and keep on low heat.

To serve: Place each dipping ingredient on a wooden skewer and dip into this wonderful cheese fonduta.

WHITE CHEDDAR FONDUTA

Fondue is claimed to be of Swiss origin. In fact it is from the Piedmont region. It is a great party dish for gatherings. Fonduta is simple and fun. Prepare all the dipping ingredients and cover until ready to serve.

Prep time: 10 min. Serves 6-8

Ingredients:

1 clove	garlic, peeled
1-1/2 cups	calvados liqueur (or apple juice)
2 pounds	white Vermont cheddar, cut into small pieces or grated
2 tablespoons	flour
1/2 teaspoon	pepper
1/2 teaspoon	nutmeg

For dipping:

1 baguette	French bread cut into cubes
2 medium	apples, cut into cubes
2 medium	pears, cut into cubes

Rub a 2-quart fondue pot with garlic. Pour calvados in pot and bring to a simmer over medium high heat. Place cheese with flour, pepper and nutmeg in the food processor. Process until cheese is finely chopped. Add cheese mixture to Calvados. Cook by stirring constantly in a figure-eight pattern until cheese is melted.

To serve: Place each dipping ingredient on a skewer, arrange in a large pitcher or vase and dip into Fonduta.

BRIE THYME FONDUTA

Fonduta, " Fondua," is a Piedmontese fondue. It is originally from the Piedmont region of Northern Italy. Fonduta or Fondue means to melt. The shepards used to dip bread into melted cheese when they came home cold and hungry. Wooden skewers are recommended rather than metal fondue forks in order to maintain sanitary conditions.

Prep time: 10 min. Serves 6-8

Ingredients:

1-1/2 cups	white wine (Chardonnay, Fume Blanc, Pinot Grigio or Chenin Blanc)
2 pounds	Brie, rind removed, cut into 1 inch pieces
2 tablespoons	flour
3/4 cup	thyme leaves, chopped

For dipping:

1 pound	mushrooms, washed and dried
1 pound	small red potatoes, boiled and peeled
8 ounces	ham, cubed into bite sizes
4 cups	French bread, cubed into bite sizes

In a 2-quart fondue pot, heat white wine on medium heat and bring to a boil. Remove from heat.

Toss Brie with flour to coat all pieces. Place Brie in the fondue pot, stirring constantly in a figure-eight pattern until Brie melts. Add chopped thyme, stir together and remove from heat.

To serve: Place mushrooms, potatoes, ham and bread on wooden skewers. Arrange skewers in a large pitcher or vase. Dip into the fonduta.

MEDITERRANEAN TOMATO BAGNA

Bagna means bath or dipping broth. Everyone who tastes this recipe seems to love it. The act of dipping food into the broth is called bagna. If you have leftover tomato bagna, use as a sauce over pasta.

Prep time: 10 min. Cook time: 15 min. Serves 6-8

Ingredients:

1 tablespoon	olive oil
2 cloves	garlic, peeled and crushed
2 cups	Marinara Sauce (see recipe under Pasta)
3 tablespoons	tomato paste
1 cup	port wine
1/2 cup	Parmesan Reggiano cheese, grated
1 cup	basil leaves, chopped
For dipping:	
1 pound	chicken, cooked <u>or</u> Italian sausage, cut into 1 inch pieces
1 pound	cheddar cheese, yellow or white, cut into 1 inch cubes
1 loaf	Foccacia bread, cut into 1 inch cubes

Place olive oil in a 2-quart fondue pot. Heat on top of stove. Remove and add crushed garlic, marinara sauce, tomato paste and port wine. Stir together until well blended. Cook on medium low heat. Add grated Parmesan Reggiano, stirring constantly in a figure-eight pattern until cheese is completely melted. Remove from heat and add basil.

To serve: Place each dipping ingredient on wooden skewers. Arrange the prepared skewers in a pitcher or long vase. Dip into the Tomato Bagna.

MEAT OR CHICKEN BAGNA

The Piedmont region is well known for its broths. This bagna not only tastes great but it is also healthy, since instead of oil, a broth is used for the cooking of the meat and chicken.

Prep time: 10 min. Serves 4 - 6

Ingredients:

2 tablespoons	olive oil
2 medium	shallots, peeled and finely chopped
1 clove	garlic, peeled and crushed
3 cups	chicken broth
1/2 teaspoon	nutmeg
2 tablespoons	lemon juice
4 tablespoons	fresh thyme leaves, chopped

For dipping:

12 ounces	chicken breast, cut into 1 inch cubes
12 ounces	filet mignon, cut into 1 inch cubes

In a 2-quart fondue pot, heat olive oil. Add chopped shallots, crushed garlic, chicken broth and nutmeg. Cook over low heat. Simmer for 10 minutes. Add lemon juice and thyme.

Salt and pepper meats. Heat broth and keep at boiling point.

To serve: Place each cube of chicken and beef on a skewer and dip into boiling broth until cooked. Serve with Mustard Cream Dip, Horseradish Mayonnaise Dip, Fennel Dip or Roasted Red Pepper Dip.

ROASTED RED PEPPER DIP

Roasted Red Pepper dip can be used on toast to make bruschettas. Great as a sauce on grilled chicken, shish kebab, fish or shrimp. Can be used as a dip for Seafood Dill Bagna or Meat or Chicken Bagna.

Prep time: 10 min. Makes 1-1/2 cups

Ingredients:

1 (8 ounce)	jar roasted red peppers
2 cloves	garlic, peeled and crushed
2 tablespoons	balsamic vinegar
1/4 cup	extra virgin olive oil
salt and pepper	to taste

Drain roasted red peppers and place in a food processor bowl. Add garlic, balsamic vinegar, olive oil, salt and pepper. Process until pureed. Place in a bowl and serve.

SEAFOOD DILL BAGNA

This bagna is excellent for dipping shrimp and scallops.

Prep time: 10 min. Cook time: 15 min. Serves 6-8

Ingredients:

1 stalk	leek, washed and finely diced (white part only)
2 tablespoons	olive oil
2 cups	vegetable stock
1/2 cup	white wine
1/4 cup	dill, chopped
2 tablespoons	lemon juice

For dipping:

1 pound	medium sized shrimp, raw and peeled
1 pound	scallops, raw.

Place diced leek in warm water. Lift leek from water. Repeat this process several times until the water in the bottom is clear and free of sand.

Place olive oil in 2-quart fondue pot. Sauté leek, add vegetable stock and white wine. Bring to a boil, then simmer on low heat. Add chopped dill and lemon juice.

To serve: Place raw, peeled shrimp and scallops on wooden skewers. Dip into Seafood Dill Bagna until cooked. Serve with Fennel Dip and Roasted Red Pepper Dip.

Apricot Bagna, see recipe on page 81.

APRICOT BAGNA

The Apricot Bagna can be served at room temperature. It is everyone's favorite. Leftovers can be frozen or used to poach fruits.

Prep time: 10 min. Serves 6

Ingredients:

1 cup	fresh apricots, or canned apricots, chopped
2 cups	apricot nectar
2 tablespoons	apricot preserve
1 tablespoon	brandy or cognac (optional) or 1 tablespoon rose water
For dipping:	
cubes of	angel food cake
2 large	bananas, sliced
18 pieces	amaretto cookies

In a food processor, place all ingredients and process until smooth. Place in a wide-mouthed fondue pot. Do not use heat under the pot.

To serve: Skewer your choice of dipping ingredients and enjoy!

CHOCOLATE BAGNA

For chocolate lovers this is a sinful temptation. I prefer imported chocolate. Dried fruits can be substituted in place of fresh.

Prep time: 10 min. Serves 6

Ingredients:

9 ounces	Belgian chocolate, broken into small pieces
1/2 cup	heavy cream
1 tablespoon	orange liqueur
For dipping:	
12 one-inch cubes	angel food cake
12 large	marshmallows
12 large	strawberries
1 medium	pear, apple, or other seasonal fruit, cubed

Cut chocolate into small pieces. Heat heavy cream and stir in chocolate until melted and smooth. Add orange liqueur and stir.

To serve: Place cubes of cake, marshmallows and fruits onto wooden skewers and dip into chocolate.

FENNEL DIP

This dip is excellent for Seafood Dill Bagna or Meat or Chicken Bagna.

Prep time: 15 min. Makes 1 cup

Ingredients:

1 bulb	fennel, washed and cut into 1/4 inch pieces
3/4 cup	ketchup
1 tablespoon	Worcestershire sauce
1/4 cup	mayonnaise
1 teaspoon	relish
1 teaspoon	Dijon mustard
2 teaspoons	horseradish

Place fennel in a food processor. Add ketchup, Worcestershire sauce, mayonnaise, relish, Dijon mustard and horseradish. Process until well blended.

Spoon into a serving bowl.

HORSERADISH MAYONNAISE DIP

Horseradish Mayonnaise Dip can be used with roast beef or grilled chicken. This can also be used for Meat or Chicken Bagna.

Prep time: 10 min. Makes 1 cup

Ingredients:

1 cup	mayonnaise
1 tablespoon	horseradish
1 tablespoon	Worcestershire sauce
salt and pepper	

Mix all ingredients together. Place in a serving bowl.

LEMON DIP

The Lemon Dip is excellent for Seafood Bagna. Also it can also be served with Chicken and Meat Bagna.

Prep time: 10 min. Makes 1-1/2 cups

Ingredients:

1 cup	crème fraîche or low-fat sour cream
1 tablespoon	capers
2 tablespoons	lemon juice
1 tablespoon	lemon zest
1 teaspoon	Herbes de Provençe
salt and pepper	to taste

Mix crème fraîche or low-fat sour cream with capers, lemon juice, lemon zest, Herbes de Provençe, salt and pepper to taste. Place dip in a serving bowl.

MUSTARD CREAMY DIP

A great dip for bagnas, especially the Meat or Chicken Bagna.

Prep time: 10 min. Makes 1 cup

Ingredients:

2 tablespoons	chives, chopped
1 cup	crème fraîche or sour cream
1 tablespoon	Dijon mustard
salt and pepper	to taste

Add cream, mustard, salt and pepper to the chopped chives. Mix thoroughly, place in a bowl and serve.

Jeanette admiring the crayfish at the Farmer's Market.

Farmer's Market finds Jeanette examing fish.

Farmer's Market and Jeanette with the Sunflowers.

Jeanette finds a variety of eggplant at the Farmer's Market.

FISH

STEAMED HALIBUT

The Steamed Halibut is a quick meal, also very low in fat and calories. Fennel goes excellent with fish.

Prep time: 20 min. Cook time: 15 min. Serves 4

Ingredients:

4 (6 ounce)	pieces of halibut (grouper)
4 leaves	Swiss chard
1 tablespoon	olive oil
salt and pepper	to taste
Steaming Broth:	
1 small	head of fennel, sliced, saving leaves
2 cloves	garlic, peeled and chopped
4 medium	lemons, peeled and sliced
2 medium	tomatoes, diced
1 medium	onion, peeled and chopped
4 cups	water
salt and pepper	to taste
1/2 teaspoon	saffron
1 tablespoon	olive oil

Steaming Broth: Combine the sliced fennel, garlic, lemon, tomatoes, onion, water, salt and pepper in a 6-quart pot. Bring to a quick boil. Add saffron. Let it steep into the broth.

Place Swiss chard leaves on a steamer. Add fish and brush with olive oil. Top with fennel leaves, salt and pepper. Place the steamer on top of the pan. Cover tightly and steam the fillets over simmering liquid for 12–14 minutes, depending on the thickness. Test by touch and sight. The fish should feel firm, not hard or rubbery and the flesh should just begin to yield to pressure. To be sure slide a knife into one fillet and separate to look for rawness. Remove steamed fish, and place on a serving platter. Puree the steaming broth. Top fish with puree of steaming broth.

AGAVE GRILLED SALMON

Agave is the fermented pulp of the plant from which tequila is made. Leftover salmon is great for making salads, also salmon cakes.

Prep time: 15 min. Cook time: 12 min. - 20 min. Serves 6

Marinate several hours or overnight

Ingredients:

6 (8 ounce)	salmon fillets, boned and skin removed
2 tablespoons	olive oil

Tequila Orange Marinade:

1 cup	orange juice
4 tablespoons	fresh chopped dill
1/2 cup	melted butter or olive oil
3 tablespoons	white tequila
salt and pepper	to taste
3 teaspoons	balsamic vinegar

In a food processor bowl, place all ingredients for marinade. Hold the balsamic vinegar until salmon is cooked. Process all ingredients together.

Place salmon fillets in a glass pan. Pour marinade on top and let stand for at least one hour or preferably overnight.

Cut a 15x18 inch piece of heavy aluminum foil, butter or oil generously. Drain salmon, reserve marinade. Preheat grill to medium heat. Place pieces of salmon on oiled or buttered aluminum foil, take to grill, cook on medium heat for 12 minutes for fillets less than 1 inch thick, 20 minutes for fillets over an inch thick.

Place reserved marinade in a saucepan. Add balsamic vinegar, heat over medium heat and bring to a quick boil. Turn off the heat.

Place cooked salmon fillets on a serving platter, drizzle extra marinade on top, and serve.

See photo on page 164

SALMON FILLETS WITH PISTACHIOS AND PINE NUTS

This recipe is so quick to make. The crust on the salmon is incredibly tasty. Panko is Japanese bread crumbs available in the oriental section of most supermarkets.

Prep time: 10 min. Cook time: 20 min. Serves 2

Preheat oven to 400°

Ingredients:

2 (4 ounce)	salmon fillets
1 teaspoon	olive oil
1 tablespoon	pine nuts, chopped
1 tablespoon	pistachio nuts, chopped
3 tablespoons	fresh thyme leaves
1 tablespoon	Asiago cheese, grated
1/2 cup	Panko bread crumbs
salt and pepper	to taste

Chop in the food processor pine nuts, pistachio nuts and thyme. Remove and place in a dish. Add grated Asiago cheese, Panko bread crumbs, salt and pepper. Brush oil on both sides of the salmon fillets. Carefully pat the nut mixture over the surface of each fillet, pressing lightly to stick. Place fish on a baking sheet lined with parchment paper. Place in the oven and bake for 20 minutes. Remove and drizzle with leftover olive oil.

Ling Cod Fillet Swirl, see recipe on page 90.

LING COD FILLET SWIRL

Florentine method is the preparation of fish when spinach is included. Great recipe to prepare ahead. Assemble and refrigerate. Bake prior to serving.

Prep time: 20 min. Cook time: 35 min. Serves 4

Preheat oven to 375°

Ingredients:

4 (6 ounce)	fillets, ling cod
1 tablespoon	olive oil

Dilled Florentine Filling:

1/2 medium	onion, peeled, cut into 8ths
1 bunch	fresh spinach, stems removed, washed and dried
1 bunch	fresh dill, stems removed, washed and dried
1 tablespoon	olive oil
1/2 cup	white wine
1/2 cup	breadcrumbs
1/4 cup	milk
salt and pepper	to taste

Dilled Florentine Sauce:

1/2 cup	Dilled Florentine Filling
1/4 cup	milk
1/8 cup	blackberries, fresh or frozen and thawed
1 tablespoon	brandy
2 teaspoons	balsamic vinegar

Chop onion, spinach and dill in a food processor or blender until pureed. In a sauté pan, heat 1 tablespoon olive oil. Add the pureed mixture and sauté for one minute. Add wine. Reserve 1/2 cup of mixture for sauce.

To the remaining Dilled Florentine Filling add the breadcrumbs, milk, salt and pepper.

Wash and dry fillets. Remove any visible bones. Run fingers through fillets to check for bones. If there are bones, pull them out with tweezers. Brush each fillet with oil on both sides. Salt and pepper each. Divide filling into 4 equal portions. Place one portion of the Dilled Florentine Filling on each fillet, and roll in a swirl. Oil a 9 x 13 inch ovenproof baking dish. Place rolled cod swirls in it, seam side down. Bake for 35 minutes.

In a food processor, place the reserved 1/2 cup Dilled Florentine Filling with milk, blackberries, brandy and balsamic vinegar. Process until well pureed. Heat.

To serve: Place fillets on a plate and top with sauce.

See photo on page 89

TROUT EN PAPIOTTE WITH PISTOU SAUCE

Pistou means pounded. The sauce is made when basil, garlic and olive oil are pureed together. This recipe can be made ahead. Refrigerate and cook the same day.

Prep time: 40 min. Cook time: 50 min. Serves 4

Preheat oven to 450°

Ingredients:

Pistou Sauce:

12 cloves	garlic, peeled and crushed
4 cups	fresh basil, washed, stems removed
1/2 cup	olive oil
4 (8 ounce)	whole trout
salt and pepper	to taste
4 sprigs	fresh rosemary
4 dried	bay leaves
1 head	bok choy, washed, stems removed and set aside

Tomato Pistou Topping:

8 medium	plum tomatoes, diced
2 medium	red or yellow peppers, seeded and diced
1 medium	onion, peeled and diced
1 cup	bok choy stems, diced
2/3 cup	pistou sauce
3 tablespoons	pine nuts
1 teaspoon	balsamic vinegar
freshly squeezed	lemon juice to taste

In a food processor, place garlic and basil, process. Pour in oil slowly and process to paste consistency. Add salt and pepper to taste. Transfer to a glass bowl or jar. Keep the pistou sauce covered in the refrigerator for one day or freeze up to 6 months.

Boil water with a drop of olive oil and salt. Blanch bok choy leaves and stems until wilted. Rinse with cold water to retain color. Wash each fish, cutting off the head and tail and trim the fins. Cut a sheet of parchment paper, large enough to comfortably wrap each fish. Salt and pepper fish. Place 1 teaspoon of pistou sauce in the cavity of each fish and spread 1 teaspoon on the outside. Place the bay leaves and rosemary inside each fish. Wrap each trout with a bok choy leaf. Line the baking dish with the parchment paper making sure it is large enough to overlap and cover fish. Place trout wrapped with bok choy leaf on top of parchment paper and overlap paper covering the fish.

Place in center of oven and bake for 35 minutes. Turn off oven and cover with aluminum foil.

Tomato Pistou Topping: Remove 1 tablespoon of oil from pistou sauce and place in a large sauté pan. Add tomatoes, peppers, onion and bok choy and cook together, stirring constantly on high heat for 10 minutes. Add pistou sauce, pine nuts and 1 teaspoon balsamic vinegar. Stir and cook for 5 minutes. Adjust seasoning if needed.

To serve: Place fish on a platter and top with Tomato Pistou Sauce.

See photo on page 92

Trout En Papiotte with Pistou Sauce, see recipe on page 91.

POULTRY

APPLE BLUE CHEESE CHICKEN ROULADES

This recipe can be prepared ahead, then sauté the roulades just before serving.

Prep time: 1 hr. Cook time: 20-30 min. Serves 6

Ingredients:

4 (6 ounce)	chicken breasts, boneless, skinless
salt and pepper	to taste
Apple Stuffing:	
1/2 cup	crumbled blue cheese
3 tablespoons	chèvre (goat cheese)
1 tablespoon	calvados (apple brandy)
1/3 cup	pistachio nuts, chopped
2 medium	apples, peeled and finely diced
Coating:	
2/3 cup	pistachio nuts, finely chopped
3/4 cup	Panko bread crumbs
1 tablespoon	Herbes de Provençe
salt and pepper	to taste
3 medium	egg whites, beaten
3 tablespoons	melted butter

Apple Stuffing: In a bowl mix blue cheese with chèvre and calvados, then add chopped pistachio nuts and diced apples. Mix well and refrigerate.

Coating: Mix chopped pistachio nuts, Panko, Herbes de Provençe, salt and pepper. Place in a shallow dish and set aside.

Chicken Roulades: Wash chicken breasts. Pat dry. Lay each chicken breast with the smooth side down on a sheet of plastic wrap larger than the chicken breast and cover with another plastic sheet. With a heavy object or mallet, flatten the breasts evenly to 1/4 inch thick. Remove the top sheet of plastic and generously salt and pepper the breasts.

Spread a quarter of the stuffing onto each breast to within 1/2 inch of the edges. Using the bottom sheet of plastic wrap to help lift the breast, fold about 1/2 inch of each long side into the filling. Press down firmly. Again using the wrap as a guide, roll the breasts starting with the narrow end. Keep the folded edges tucked in. Roll tightly resembling a sausage. Repeat same process for each chicken breast. Place each roulade seam side down on a plate and refrigerate.

Roll each roulade in egg whites to cover completely. Reserve one tablespoon of coating for garnish. Roll in the coating mixture. Make sure the pieces are well coated. Press the coating with your hands. Cover.

In a sauté pan, heat 3 tablespoons of butter over medium heat until the butter foams. Add the roulades seam side down; cook over medium heat turning them every few minutes. Cook until the crust is well browned and the chicken feels firm when pressed, about 15 to 20 minutes.

Let roulades rest prior to cutting in slices. Garnish with 1 tablespoon of coating.

CHICKEN BREAST MARSALA

This recipe is easy and fast to make. Just serve it with a salad and any desired accompaniment such as rice or mashed potatoes.

Prep time: 10 min. Cook time: 20 min. Serves 4

Ingredients:

4 (6 ounce)	chicken breasts, boneless, skinless, butterflied, pounded
1 tablespoon	olive oil
1 medium	lemon, juiced and zested
1/2 cup	Marsala wine or apple juice
8 leaves	fresh basil, washed, stacked, rolled and julienned (chiffonade)
salt and pepper	to taste

Wash and pat chicken dry. Butterfly and pound with a heavy object by placing plastic wrap directly on the chicken. Pound until 1/4 inch thick.

Place olive oil in a sauté pan. Brown pounded chicken quickly on high heat. Cook 4 minutes on one side. Turn chicken over, and continue to cook for an additional 4 minutes. Add the lemon zest, juice of the lemon and deglaze with Marsala wine. Add basil, salt and pepper.

Olive Lemon Chicken, see recipe on page 97.

OLIVE LEMON CHICKEN

This recipe is of Moroccan origin. It is a great dish to make in a clay pot and also an excellent dish that can be prepared ahead of time and served for a crowd.

Prep time: 20 min. Cook time: 1 hr. Serves 4

Preheat oven to 375°; or if using clay pot, do not preheat oven.

Ingredients:

1 medium	red onion, peeled and chopped
3 cloves	garlic, peeled and chopped
2 tablespoons	olive oil
6 pieces	chicken drumsticks, thighs or breasts
1 teaspoon	cumin
1 teaspoon	paprika
2 teaspoons	ginger, freshly grated or sliced
salt and pepper	to taste
3/4 cup	chicken broth
1/4 teaspoon	ground tumeric or saffron
1/2 bunch	cilantro, washed, dried, stems removed and chopped
1/2 bunch	flat leaf parsley, washed, dried, stems removed and chopped
1 medium	lemon, peeled, scrubbed and sliced
1 cup	green olives, pitted
1 medium	lemon, juiced

Place onion and garlic in food processor. Add oil and process. Remove and place in a bowl. Combine cumin, paprika, grated ginger, salt and pepper. Mix onion, garlic and all the spices together and toss with chicken pieces. Place in a roasting pan or clay pot.

Heat broth and steep saffron or tumeric until broth is quite warm. Let cool to room temperature. Add steeped broth to chicken mixture. Combine part of the cilantro, parsley and pitted olives with chicken mixture and mix well. Save some cilantro, parsley, and pitted olives for garnish.

Cover and place in preheated oven. (If using a clay pot, do not preheat the oven). Bake at 375° for 30 minutes. Uncover and add lemon slices by placing them between chicken pieces. Add pitted olives and lemon juice. Mix well, and continue baking for another 30 minutes.

Remove from heat and serve.

CHICKEN KOFTA KEBAB

Kofta Kebab is a great crowd pleaser when having a get together. It can be prepared the day before then just grill prior to serving. Also a good recipe to take along on a picnic or camping trip.

Prep time: 20 min. Cook time: 20 min. Serves 4-6

Ingredients:

1 medium	onion, peeled and cut into 8ths
1 large	tomato, cut into 8ths
2 cloves	garlic, peeled and crushed
1/4 bunch	Italian parsley, stems removed, washed and dried
1 teaspoon	salt
1/4 teaspoon	pepper
1/4 teaspoon	allspice
1/8 teaspoon	cinnamon
1 pound	ground meat (beef, lamb or chicken)
1 tablespoon	olive oil for brushing grill
16 large	bamboo skewers

Soak bamboo skewers a couple of hours or preferably overnight.

In a food processor bowl or blender, place onion, tomato, garlic, parsley, salt, pepper, allspice, and cinnamon. Process all together until finely chopped.

Place meat in a mixing bowl. Add all other chopped ingredients. Knead well to incorporate meat and vegetables.

Oil grill, and preheat to medium heat for at least 10 minutes.

Divide the meat mixture into 16 portions. Wrap each meat mixture around a bamboo skewer. Press firmly to hold. If needed, wet hands to help meat adhere to skewers. Another option is to roll the meat mixture into the shape of a sausage. Keep chilled until time to grill.

Place kebab on the oiled grill and cook for approximately 8 minutes on each side. Test one to the doneness desired. Serve with Pita bread or rice as a side dish.

CHICKEN WITH CURRY, APPLES, AND BANANAS

This recipe is of Caribbean origin. It is great for summer entertaining. Serve with rice or cooked orzo.

Prep time: 20 min. Cook time: 45 min. to 1 hr. Serves 4

Ingredients:

2 tablespoons	olive oil
6 pieces	chicken (2 drumsticks, 2 thighs, 2 breasts)
2 medium	shallots, peeled and chopped
2 cloves	garlic, peeled and crushed
4 teaspoons	curry powder
salt and pepper	to taste
2 large	red apples, unpeeled and sliced into large pieces
1/2 cup	chicken broth
2 medium	bananas
1/2 cup	crème fraîche
1/2 cup	sesame seeds or sunflower seeds
1/2 medium	lemon, juiced

Wash and dry chicken pieces. Place olive oil in large pot. Add chicken, and sauté until light brown. Add shallots and garlic. Cook over low heat for about 20 minutes browning chicken on all sides. Sprinkle with curry powder and mix together. Add salt and pepper. Add to the chicken, apples, chicken broth and bring to a boil. Cover and simmer on low heat for 25 to 30 minutes until chicken is done.

Just prior to serving, peel and cut bananas into 2 inch slices. Add to chicken mixture. Add crème fraîche and sesame or sunflower seeds. Stir gently. Cook on low heat for 5 minutes. Add lemon juice and stir gently.

Serve with rice and garnish with mango and pineapple slices.

See photo on page 100

Chicken With Curry, Apples, and Bananas, see recipe on page 99.

RISOTTO ROASTED CHICKEN

This risotto dish can be served without stuffing chicken. Just bake or grill whole chicken or pieces of chicken.

Prep time: 20 min. Cook time: 1 hr. 45 min. Serves 6

Preheat oven to 375°

Ingredients:

Risotto Stuffing:

1 large	onion, peeled and chopped
4 cloves	garlic, peeled and crushed
1 tablespoon	olive oil
1 pound	ground meat (beef, lamb, veal, turkey or chicken)
salt and pepper	to taste
1 teaspoon	allspice
1 cup	uncooked long grain rice
2 cups	chicken broth
1 tablespoon	olive oil
1/2 cup	pine nuts or slivered almonds

Chicken:

1 (4-5 pound)	whole chicken
3 cloves	garlic, peeled and crushed
salt and pepper	to taste
1 teaspoon	allspice
1 medium	lemon, juiced
2 tablespoons	olive oil
2 tablespoons	fresh rosemary chopped

Optional sauce:

1/2 cup	water or broth for deglazing

Place olive oil in a 6-quart pot. Sauté meat, add chopped onion, garlic, salt, pepper, allspice, rice and broth. Cover. Bring to a boil. Reduce heat and simmer for 20 minutes until rice forms little holes.

Sauté pine nuts reserving 2 tablespoons for garnish. Add pine nuts to rice. Remove from heat and cool. This can be done a day ahead.

Clean chicken well. Remove fat by lifting skin and then letting water run to wash chicken thoroughly. Wash hands, knives, scissors and cutting board with soap and water before proceeding to the next step to prevent salmonella.

Make a paste with crushed garlic, salt, pepper, allspice, lemon juice, olive oil and chopped rosemary. Rub paste inside and outside of chicken.

Make sure the stuffing temperature is the same as the chicken temperature. Stuff chicken with rice mixture and close cavity with skewers. Place in a roasting pan. Cover and bake for 1 hour. Remove cover and continue baking for at least 45 minutes until the thermometer reads 180°. Remove chicken from oven and place on a serving platter. Discard skewers. With the aid of a spoon, remove stuffing and place around chicken. Garnish with pine nuts and rosemary.

Optional sauce: Remove fat from roasting pan. Deglaze by adding 1/2 cup water or broth and scrub hard with a wooden spoon to loosen concentrated juices. Stir contents of pan and cook over low heat for five minutes.

POULET A L'ORANGE
ORANGE ROASTED CHICKEN

This recipe is low in fat and great when cooked in a clay pot. Stays nice and moist.

Prep time: 30 min. Cook time: 60 min. Serves 4-6

Preheat oven to 375°

Ingredients:

1 (4–5 pound)	roasting chicken, washed and dried
2 medium	oranges, washed, peeled and sliced into rings
1 medium	onion, peeled and sliced into rings.
1 (14 ounce)	can chicken broth

Mixture:

2 medium	oranges, juiced
1 tablespoon	mustard
2 tablespoons	orange marmalade jam
1 tablespoon	fresh ginger, grated
1 tablespoon	flour
1 tablespoon	Herbes de Provençe
salt and pepper	to taste

Remove all fat under skin from breast, legs and back.

Mixture: Combine the orange juice, mustard, orange marmalade, grated ginger, flour, Herbes de Provençe, salt and pepper.

Place chicken in a roasting pan. Lift the skin and spread the mixture evenly making sure not to break the skin. Place a couple of the sliced oranges and onions under the breast skin and also between the legs. Pour broth over the chicken and place the remaining orange slices and onion rings on top of the chicken. Tie the legs together with string. Cook covered in preheated oven for 35 minutes. Uncover and continue cooking for an additional 25 minutes. Remove from oven and serve.

STUFFED CHICKEN WITH LEEK AND MUSHROOM

The stuffing can be done a day ahead and refrigerated until ready to use. The stuffing is great as a side dish or an accompaniment to meat or fish.

Prep time: 30 min. Cook time: 1hr. 45 min. Serves 6

Preheat oven to 375°

Stuffing:

2 medium	leeks, white part only, washed and sliced
1-1/2 pounds	mushrooms, cleaned and sliced
3 cloves	garlic, peeled and crushed
3 tablespoons	olive oil
2 tablespoons	fresh basil leaves, chopped
2 tablespoons	fresh thyme leaves, chopped
1 teaspoon	allspice
salt and pepper	to taste
1 cup	uncooked basmati rice
2 cups	chicken broth
1 tablespoon	olive oil
1 cup	pistachio nuts

Chicken:

1 (4 - 5 pound)	whole chicken
3 cloves	garlic, peeled and crushed
1 tablespoon	allspice
6 sprigs	fresh rosemary, chopped
1 medium	lemon, juiced
1 tablespoon	olive oil
salt and pepper	to taste

Garnish:

2 tablespoons	pistachio nuts
2 sprigs	fresh rosemary
2 sprigs	fresh thyme

Optional Sauce:

1/2 cup	water or broth for deglazing

Slice leeks and soak them in warm water. Lift leeks from water and place in a colander and run cold water over them. Rinse with cold water several times until no sand is visible.

Heat oil in a 4-quart pan fitted with a lid. Sauté leeks, mushrooms, garlic, basil, and thyme. Add allspice, salt, pepper, rice and broth. Cover and bring to boil. Simmer for 20 minutes until little holes form on top of rice. Remove and let cool. This can be done a day ahead.

Sauté pistachio nuts in 1 tablespoon of olive oil. Reserve 2 tablespoons of the nuts for garnish.

Clean chicken well. Remove fat by lifting skin, then let water run to wash chicken thoroughly. Wash hands, knives, scissors and cutting board with soap and water before proceeding to the next step to prevent salmonella. Pat chicken dry and set aside.

Combine crushed garlic, allspice, chopped rosemary, lemon juice, olive oil, salt and pepper; mix together. Lift chicken skin and rub inside and outside of chicken with mixture.

The temperature of the cavity and neck of the chicken should be the same as the stuffing. If temperature varies, salmonella may occur.

Stuff chicken cavity and neck with cooled stuffing. Secure with skewers to close the cavity and neck and place stuffed chicken in a roasting pan. If there is any remaining stuffing, save and heat prior to serving. Cover stuffed chicken and cook for 1 hour. Uncover and cook for another 45 minutes or test with thermometer which should read 180°. Remove from oven and place on a serving platter.

Remove skewers. With the aid of a spoon, remove stuffing and place on a platter. Place cooked chicken on top. Garnish with pistachio nuts, rosemary and thyme.

Optional sauce: Remove fat from roasting pan. Deglaze by adding 1/2 cup water or broth and scrub hard with a wooden spoon to loosen concentrated juices. Stir contents of pan and cook over low heat for five minutes.

Stuffed Chicken with Leek and Mushroom

MAIN COURSES

CASSOULET (KA-SOO-LAY) WITH DUCK AND CHICKEN SAUSAGE

Cassoulet is a bean stew that originated in Languedoc. It is prepared with a variety of meats in an earthenware dish, which used to be known as the Cassole d'Issel. The dish derives its name from this beginning. There are a variety of cassoulets and they differ according to individual tastes. This dish is great on a cold evening. The smell of cassoulet cooking is robust. It can be prepared ahead of time and reheated in the oven. The beans, vegetables, browning the duck and sausages can be done the day before and refrigerated until ready to assemble.

Prep time: 3 hrs. Cook time: 3 hrs. Serves: 6-8

Preheat oven to 375°

Ingredients:

2 cups	dry white beans
1 cup	carrots, peeled and diced
1 cup	onion, peeled and diced
1 cup	celery, diced
1 cup	parsnips, peeled and diced
5 large	tomatoes, finely chopped
1 tablespoon	olive oil
1 cup	dry white wine
4 cups	chicken broth
1 Bouquet Garni	(see recipe)
6 cloves	garlic, peeled
4 pounds	duck, cut into 8 pieces
2 tablespoons	duck fat, reserved
1 pound	chicken or veal sausages
1 cup	Panko bread crumbs
1/4 cup	fresh parsley, chopped
salt and pepper	to taste
3 sprigs	thyme for garnish

Gremolade:

1/2 cup	parsley, finely chopped
2 cloves	garlic, peeled and crushed
1 large	lemon, zested

Gremolade: Mix all gremolade ingredients together and refrigerate until ready to use.

Spread dried beans on a baking sheet and sort through them. Remove any stones, dirt, or shriveled beans. Rinse and drain.

Heat 1 tablespoon olive oil in a large 6-quart casserole pan. Add diced vegetables, cover and simmer for 15 minutes. Deglaze casserole dish with wine and simmer for one minute. Remove from pan and set aside.

Assemble Bouquet Garni. Using the same pan, add the rinsed beans and 3-1/2 cups of chicken broth so it covers the beans. Bring to a boil. Cook beans until slightly tender. Add Bouquet Garni. Reduce heat. Cover and simmer 30 minutes until the beans start to get tender. Drain, reserving liquid. Cool.

In a food processor, process garlic cloves until finely chopped. Add 1/2 cup of chicken broth and process until blended. Set aside.

Season duck pieces with some salt and pepper. Heat a large sauté pan. Sear the duck in batches, skin side down. Cook until golden, and then remove. When finished pour off all but 2 tablespoons of fat and return to burner. Add sausages to pan, and cook until brown. Remove sausages and set aside.

Deglaze sauté pan with garlic broth mixture. Bring to a boil for one minute scraping up bits from the bottom.

In a bowl, combine breadcrumbs with chopped parsley, salt and pepper to taste. Set aside.

Remove Bouquet Garni from beans. Combine beans with garlic broth and vegetable mixture. Add salt and pepper to taste.

To Assemble and Bake Cassoulet: Spread half of the bean/vegetable mixture in a 6-quart casserole or ovenproof deep dish. Place 4 pieces of duck on top. Repeat layering using remaining bean mixture and duck. If any liquid remains, pour over the cassoulet.

Sprinkle 1/3 cup of breadcrumbs on top. Place the dish on a baking sheet to catch drippings. Bake for one hour. Stir crust into cassoulet. Sprinkle another 1/3 cup of breadcrumbs on top. Continue baking for another hour. Stir cassoulet a second time. Add the reserved sausages and sprinkle the top with remaining breadcrumbs. Return to oven and bake for one more hour. The cassoulet is done when the top crust is crispy and bubbly. Garnish with sprigs of thyme.

To serve: Spoon cassoulet into individual bowls. If desired, top with Gremolade.

Garden Vegetables

Terrine De Campagne – French Meatloaf, see recipe on page 110.

TERRINE DE CAMPAGNE
FRENCH MEATLOAF

The terrine is the earthenware dish in which fish, game or meat are cooked. The word terrine is also used to designate the food itself. The terrine must be completely cold before it is eaten. It can be kept for several days in perfect condition provided it is refrigerated. This is a great picnic dish or to be used for outdoor parties. Serve with baguettes, cornichons and mustard.

Prep time: 1 hr. Cook time: 1 hr. 45 min. Serves 9

Preheat oven to 350°

Ingredients:

1 pound	ground chicken or ground lamb
1 pound	ground veal or ground turkey
1/4 pound	ground pork
1 medium	onion, peeled and chopped
2 cloves	garlic, peeled and crushed
1/4 cup	thyme leaves, chopped
1/4 cup	tarragon leaves, chopped
1/2 cup	parsley, stems removed and chopped
1 teaspoon	Herbes de Provençe
1 teaspoon	nutmeg
1/4 cup	cognac or brandy
1/2 teaspoon	pepper
1 teaspoon	salt
2 large	eggs, beaten
1/4 cup	heavy cream

Filling:

2 medium	carrots, parboiled, peeled and sliced lengthwise
5 spears	asparagus, peeled and steamed
3 ounces	prosciutto, diced
4 slices	roasted red peppers, chopped
2 tablespoons	pistachio nuts

In the food processor bowl or a blender place meats, onion, garlic, thyme, tarragon, parsley, Herbes de Provençe, nutmeg, cognac or brandy, pepper, salt, eggs and heavy cream. Process or blend until all ingredients are thoroughly mixed, remove and place in another bowl. Cover and keep refrigerated.

Divide meat mixture into 3 equal portions. Place one portion of the meat mixture in the bottom of a loaf pan 10x5x3 inches. Top with strips of carrots and asparagus, alternating them. Press down lightly with palm of hand. Top with 2nd portion of meat. Sprinkle roasted peppers, proscuitto, and pistachio nuts over the meat. Cover with third portion of meat. Cut a piece of parchment paper to cover top of loaf pan.

Boil water. Fill a large pan with 1 inch water. Place covered loaf pan inside the water pan (Bain Marie). Place in oven and bake for 1 hour and 45 minutes. Test with knife or toothpick for doneness. There should be no pink color to the juices when pierced. Remove from oven. Drain fat from terrine. Let cool, release sides of terrine before inverting onto a platter.

STUFFED PORK TENDERLOIN WITH RHUBARB SAUCE

This is heavenly delicious. This recipe was one of the most popular dishes on the menu when I had my catering business. Rhubarb season is from May until July. During this time it is available in most supermarkets. Because rhubarb is difficult to find during other times, it is recommended that it be purchased and frozen. Make the rhubarb sauce first, even the day before. This dish is ideal for the holidays since you can prepare and refrigerate for the next day. Occasionally, pork tenderloin may be packaged two per package, the total weight should be between 2 to 3 pounds.

Prep time: 45 - 60 min. Cook time: 30 min. Serves 4-5

Preheat oven to 350°

Ingredients:

2 - 3 pounds	pork tenderloin
Stuffing:	
1 bunch	fresh spinach, stems removed
1 medium	leek, white part only, sliced
3/4 cup	mushrooms, sliced
1/4 cup	fresh sage leaves
2 tablespoons	butter
1 cup	Panko bread crumbs
1/2 teaspoon	nutmeg
1 small	egg
salt and pepper	to taste
Sage Paste:	
1 tablespoon	fresh sage
2 tablespoons	butter
salt and pepper	to taste
Rhubarb Sauce:	
2 cups	fresh rhubarb or 1 (14 ounce) can red cherries (if rhubarb is unavailable)
1 cup	beef broth
1 tablespoon	fresh ginger, grated
1 cup	Port wine
3 tablespoons	butter
salt and pepper	to taste

Soak spinach in warm water to remove sand, lift spinach and place in colander. Rinse with cold water, drain and dry well.

Soak sliced leek in warm water, lift leeks, wash with cold water and drain. Place spinach, mushrooms and sage in food processor, process until pureed.

Stuffing: Heat butter in a sauté pan. Sauté leeks and cook until translucent. Add the pureed spinach, mushrooms and sage mixture to the sautéed leeks. Cook on low heat for 5 minutes. Season with nutmeg, salt and pepper. Remove from heat. Add bread crumbs and mix together. Let stand until mixture cools, then add egg, mix well and set aside.

Slit the tenderloins in half lengthwise. Butterfly each tenderloin so that they lay open, flat and even. If needed, place a plastic wrap on top and pound to flatten the tenderloins. Divide the stuffing in half, place 1/2 of the stuffing in the center of each flattened tenderloin. Roll and tie with string at 1-inch intervals. Wrap the tenderloin rolls tightly with plastic wrap and refrigerate until ready to cook.

Sage paste: Place all ingredients for sage paste into a food processor bowl and process until pureed. Rub tenderloin with sage paste.

Sear each rubbed tenderloin in a sauté pan until the outside is quite brown. Place the seared tenderloins on a baking dish, bake for 8 -10 minutes. Check with a meat thermometer for doneness, the temperature should register 150°. Continue to bake until ready. Remove from oven and let tenderloin rest for 5 minutes.

Rhubarb Sauce: Place all the ingredients for the rhubarb sauce in a sauce pan. Bring to a soft boil, reduce heat, simmer until sauce is reduced and thickened.

To serve: Slice stuffed pork tenderloin with a sharp knife and top with the rhubarb sauce.

Stuffed Pork Tenderloin with Rhubarb Sauce, see recipe on page 112.

OXTAILS UBRIACO – DRUNKEN OXTAILS WITH CANNELLINI, MUSHROOMS AND PENNETTE

Oxtails do not come from oxen but from beef. Oxtails are chunks from the tail of the cattle. When oxtails are braised, the collagen is released which renders a rich and textured sauce. This recipe is worth all the work when your guests ooh and ahh! The oxtails can be cooked the day before and refrigerated. The longer it cooks the better it tastes. It is a labor of love to see your guests drool over it. This hearty dish is a wonderful welcome on a cool fall or winter evening that is spent with family and friends.

Prep time: 45 min. | Cook time: 4-6 hrs. | Serves 6

Preheat oven to 320°

Ingredients:

6 pounds	oxtails, cut at joint, trimmed and fat removed
1 cup	flour
1/2 cup	peanut oil
2 tablespoons	olive oil
2 medium	carrots, peeled and sliced
3 medium	shallots, peeled, sliced and diced
1 medium	leek, washed and sliced
2 stalks	celery, sliced
2 (750 ml.) bottles	Chianti wine
2 cups	tomato puree
6 cups	chicken stock
4 sprigs	thyme
1 head	garlic, peeled
salt and pepper	to taste
water if needed	

Cannellini Mushroom Pennette Mixture:

1/2 pound	pennette pasta
4 tablespoons	butter or olive oil
8 ounces	portabello and crimini mushrooms, sliced
2 (15 ounce)	cans cannellini beans, drained
2 tablespoons	parsley, chopped
10 small	potatoes, boiled
2 cups	chicken stock
6 tablespoons	Parmigiano Reggiano cheese

In a large heavy braising pan, sauté the carrots, shallots, leek and celery in olive oil or butter over high heat until light brown. Add 1-1/2 bottles of wine and bring to boil. Add chicken stock, tomato puree and bring to a boil. Keep warm.

Salt and pepper the oxtails, dredge with flour, shake off excess flour. In a large sauté pan, heat peanut oil over medium heat, add oxtails and sauté until light brown. Transfer the browned oxtails to the braising pan. Discard any excess oil in the sauté pan, add the remaining wine and deglaze. Pour the deglazed liquid into the braising pan that contains the oxtails. If liquid does not cover the oxtails, add water. Bring to boil, skim off any foam that has come to the top. Reduce heat and simmer. Add thyme, garlic, salt and pepper, cover and place in preheated oven for approximately 4-6 hours until the meat almost falls off the bone.

Cannellini Mushroom Pennette Mixture: Cook pennette pasta in salted water. Meanwhile sauté mushrooms in butter, add cannellini beans, potatoes and chicken stock. Cover and simmer. When pennette is cooked, drain and add to cannellini mushroom mixture. Toss together, season with salt and pepper, then sprinkle with chopped parsley.

To serve: Place Cannellini Mushroom Pennette mixture on individual plates. Top with oxtail mixture. Drizzle oxtail sauce over the oxtails. Grate Parmigiano Reggiano cheese on top of individual plates. Enjoy!

COUSCOUS WITH CHICKEN AND LAMB

Couscous is a North African dish. The word "koskos" is an earthenware pot in which semolina is steamed. This is a great prepare ahead dish. Steam couscous just before serving. I have very fond memories associated with this dish, as I first served it for a famous Hollywood producer's party.

Prep time: 45 min. Cook time: 45 min. Serves 6

Ingredients:

1 tablespoon	olive oil
2 cloves	garlic, peeled and crushed
1 large	onion, peeled and chopped
3 pieces	chicken breast, boned, skinned and cut into 2 inch cubes
1 pound	lamb stew meat
4 cups	water
1/2 teaspoon	coriander
1/2 teaspoon	nutmeg
1 teaspoon	saffron
salt and pepper	to taste
1 pound	carrots, peeled and sliced
3 medium	zucchini, sliced
2 medium	turnips, peeled and sliced
1 (15 ounce)	can garbanzo beans, drained
2 large	lemons, unpeeled and cut into 8ths
2 cups	couscous, steamed

Harisa Sauce:

2 large	tomatoes, chopped
1 medium	hot pepper, finely diced
2 tablespoons	olive oil
1 tablespoon	red wine vinegar
salt and pepper	

Heat oil in large Dutch oven and sauté onion and garlic until soft. Add cubed chicken and cook until lightly browned. Add lamb pieces and brown. Add 4 cups of water, coriander, nutmeg, saffron, salt and pepper. Cover and let simmer until meat is tender.

Add the vegetables and garbanzo beans to the meat mixture. Cover and simmer for 25 minutes until vegetables are cooked. Add the lemon slices to the mixture during the last five minutes.

Place couscous in a steamer and using broth from the vegetables and meat mixture, steam according to package directions.

Harisa Sauce Method: Using food processor, place all ingredients in the bowl. Process together until smooth.

To serve: Place couscous on a plate, arrange meat and vegetables on top of couscous and add desired amount of Harisa Sauce over the top.

SWEET POTATO TURKEY CASSEROLE

The smell of this bubbly au gratin coming out of the oven is so appetizing. It is great on a cool winter day. This recipe is great for leftovers from Thanksgiving and can also be made ahead.

Prep time: 45 min. Cook time: 1 hr. Serves 9

Preheat oven to 375°

Ingredients:

Casserole:

2 pounds	sweet potatoes or yams, parboiled, peeled and sliced
salt and pepper	to taste
2 medium	leeks, washed and sliced
2 tablespoons	olive oil
1-1/4 pounds	ground turkey or sliced turkey
1 teaspoon	nutmeg
1 teaspoon	Herbes de Provençe
3 cups	grated Swiss Gruyère or white cheddar cheese

Velouté Sauce:

8 ounces	cream cheese
1 cup	low-fat or regular milk
1-1/2 cups	crumbled feta cheese or chèvre cheese
1 cup	chicken broth
white pepper	to taste
salt	to taste
dash of nutmeg	

Salt and pepper sweet potatoes and set aside. Place oil in a sauté pan, heat on medium low, cook turkey adding salt, pepper and nutmeg. Add leeks and sauté until turkey and leeks are cooked. Add Herbes de Provençe. Remove from heat and hold. (When using leftover cooked turkey: sauté leeks, salt, pepper, nutmeg, Herbes de Provençe and add cooked turkey stirring to reheat for a few minutes).

Velouté Sauce: Make the Velouté Sauce using a food processor or blender. Blend all ingredients until smooth.

In a 4-quart casserole or baking dish, place a little Velouté sauce at the bottom, then layer sliced sweet potatoes. Pour some sauce on the sweet potatoes and sprinkle with a little cheese. Add the turkey mixture on top of sweet potatoes. Cover with remaining sauce. Spread remaining cheese on top.

Bake for 30 to 35 minutes until contents are bubbling and surface is brown. If not serving soon, cover and keep warm in oven.

CONTEMPORARY MOLDED MOUSSAKA

Moussaka is a classical casserole, well known in Greek, Turkish and Middle Eastern cuisine. Some believe it is of Rumanian origin. Now it is made in many Eastern countries. The Greek moussaka is made with an extra thick custard topping. My Contemporary Molded Moussaka is quite picturesque. It is molded to resemble a chocolate cake.

Prep time: 45 min. Cook time: 2hrs. 45 min. Serves 8

Preheat oven to 375°

Ingredients:

4 large	eggplants
5 tablespoons	olive oil
1 tablespoon	lemon juice
3/4 cup	hot water
1 pound	ground lamb or beef
2 cloves	garlic, peeled and crushed
3 tablespoons	onion, peeled and finely chopped
1 teaspoon	cinnamon
1/2 teaspoon	allspice
3 teaspoons	salt
1/2 teaspoon	pepper
2 tablespoons	parsley, stems removed, washed, dried and chopped
2 medium	tomatoes, diced and drained
2 medium	eggs, beaten
1/2 pound	feta cheese, crumbled (save some for garnish)

Cut 3 eggplants into halves lengthwise. Run a sharp pointed knife around the inside of the skins, separating them from pulp. Score the pulp into 1/2 inch cubes, making sure not to pierce the skin. Brush eggplants with olive oil. In a large baking dish, place hot water, lemon, salt and pepper. Place eggplants scored side down. Bake covered for 45 minutes. or until eggplants feel soft to the touch. Let cool. Remove gently from pan and scoop out pulp, leaving skins intact. Place pulp on a paper towel to make sure it dries, then place in a bowl.

Cut the fourth eggplant lengthwise into quarters and carefully peel. Reserve peels and blanch them to soften. When soft, remove skin carefully and place on a paper towel to dry. Set aside to use if necessary when lining and covering the mold. Slice eggplant 1/2 inch lengthwise. Brush both sides with olive oil. Place on a baking dish and bake until done and light brown.

Place a little olive oil in a sauté pan, add ground meat and cook for a couple of minutes, then add crushed garlic and chopped onion, cinnamon and allspice. Add cooked eggplant pulp. Cook together until liquid evaporates from mixture. Remove from heat, add parsley, tomatoes, salt and pepper. Let cool, and then add 2 beaten eggs.

To assemble: Line an oiled round mold or casserole (2-1/2-quart) with eggplant skins, having the purple exterior next to the side of the mold and extended over the edges. Make sure skins overlap in a spoke fashion especially at the bottom. Start by placing a layer of sliced eggplant at the bottom, sprinkle some feta cheese and top with one inch layer of eggplant lamb mixture. Sprinkle with more feta cheese and meat mixture. Repeat until mold is filled ending with the sliced cooked eggplant on top.

Bring the skins, which extend over the side of the mold toward the center. If all skins are used, the 4th eggplant peel may be used to cover the uncovered portion. Place a parchment paper on top, then aluminum foil. Place the mold in a pan of hot water (Bain Marie) bake for 2 hours. Remove from oven and let stand 10 minutes. Carefully drain any excess liquid. Unmold onto a serving platter and serve hot with Saltsa Domato – Tomato Sauce.

"Recipes inspired by your heart and fresh from the garden can create a dish that encompasses the past and present and makes memories for the future."

—Patricia Monda

SALTSA DOMATO
TOMATO SAUCE

This sauce is Greek in origin. It is commonly used for Moussakas, stews or as a pasta sauce. Make several batches and freeze for later use.

Prep time: 20 min. Cook time: 1 hour Makes 2 cups

Ingredients:

2 tablespoons	olive oil
1 small	onion, peeled and finely chopped
2 cloves	garlic, peeled and minced
1 (4 ounce)	can tomato paste
1-1/2 cups	water
1/2 cup	red wine
1 tablespoon	brown sugar
1/2 teaspoon	salt
1/2 teaspoon	cinnamon

Sauté onion in olive oil; add garlic, tomato paste, water, wine, brown sugar, salt and cinnamon. Cover and simmer for 1 hour.

Medley Grilled Vegetables, see recipe on page 124.

SIDE DISHES

STUFATO DI VERDURE
THE GARDEN IN A POT

This sumptuous ragu dish captures all the senses and tastes of vegetables. It is a rustic dish well known in most Tuscan Villages. Every village has their own version. It is a natural dish for Italian women who cook from a garden. In Spring, it might include fava beans, artichokes and leeks; in winter, potatoes, cabbage or kale may be used. There is always onion and garlic. Olives can be used or capers, anchovies, hot pepper, wine or vinegar. Cook several hours ahead. Can be heated or eaten at room temperature. You could grate cheese or drizzle with olive oil. Serve with grilled polenta squares or Bruschetta. The Stufato di Verdure is another version of Ratatouille or Caponata.

Prep time: 30 min. Cook time: 30 min. Serves 6

Ingredients:

1/2 cup	extra virgin olive oil
3 medium	zucchini, diced
1 large	onion, peeled and diced
1 large	eggplant, peeled and diced
2 stalks	celery, preferably hearts, diced
3 cloves	garlic, peeled and crushed
1 (14 ounce)	can tomatoes, chopped, juice reserved
1 bunch	basil leaves, washed and chopped
1/3 cup	balsamic vinegar
salt and pepper	to taste

Heat oil in a large sauté pan. Place zucchini, onion, eggplant and celery sauté until lightly brown. Stir together well. Add crushed garlic, the chopped tomatoes and juice. Cook covered for 15 minutes. Add the basil. Cover and continue cooking for another 15 minutes. Remove from heat, add balsamic vinegar, salt and pepper to taste. Let stand together so flavors will blend.

EGGPLANT TOMATOES PROVENÇAL

This recipe can be prepared 2 days in advance. Leftovers are great when tossed with pasta or used in sandwiches. It is a great topping when used on bruschettas as an appetizer.

Prep time: 30 min. Cook time: 1 hr. 30 min. Serves 6

Ingredients:

2 tablespoons	olive oil
1 medium	onion, peeled and diced
2 large	eggplants, partially peeled and diced into 1 inch pieces
5 large	tomatoes, diced
8 cloves	garlic, peeled and crushed
salt and pepper	to taste
1/4 cup	balsamic vinegar
1-1/2 teaspoons	sugar
1/2 bunch	basil leaves, washed and chopped
salt and pepper	to taste
1/4 cup	pine nuts

Heat oil, sauté onion, eggplants and tomatoes. Add crushed garlic, salt and pepper, balsamic vinegar, sugar and chopped basil. Cook together for one hour and 30 minutes. Remove from heat and add pine nuts. This can be eaten cold or at room temperature.

MEDLEY GRILLED VEGETABLES

The name Medley Grilled Vegetables was inspired by the artistic medley of colors that is created when the grilled vegetables are arranged in a large platter. The leftovers are great in a sandwich or mixed in a pasta salad. If asparagus is not in season, substitute 1 stalk fennel. Other vegetables may be substituted to your liking. This marinade is great; therefore you may want to double the recipe and freeze some for a later time.

Prep time: 20 min. Cook time: 10-15 min. Serves 6

Preheat grill on high for just 5 minutes, reduce heat to medium low.

Ingredients:

4 medium	green zucchini, cut in half lengthwise
4 medium	yellow zucchini, cut in half lengthwise
10 stalks	asparagus, cleaned and trimmed
6 small	parboiled potatoes
2 medium	red peppers, cut in half
2 medium	yellow peppers, cut in half

Medley Marinade:

3 cloves	garlic, peeled and crushed
1/3 cup	balsamic vinegar or lemon juice
1 cup	olive oil
1 teaspoon	salt
1/4 teaspoon	pepper
1 teaspoon	Herbes de Provençe

Place all Medley Marinade ingredients in the food processor and process or place in a jar with a lid and shake well.

Brush vegetables with half the Medley Marinade. Save the rest to pour over the vegetables after they have been grilled, but while they are still hot.

Place vegetables directly on medium grill. Cook for 10 minutes until vegetables are al dente. Remove from grill, place on a serving platter; drizzle the saved Medley Marinade on the top while vegetables are still hot.

See photo on page 161

TURKEY CHESTNUT FOCACCIA STUFFING

This recipe is ample stuffing for a 16-pound turkey, with some leftover. Cooked chestnuts are usually available in gourmet stores. They are only available during the Holiday season. I recommend purchasing extra and freezing. The focaccia stuffing is also available in the gourmet stores and only during the Holidays. If desired, you may substitute regular bread stuffing and pistachio instead of chestnut.

Prep time: 10 min. Cook time: 10 min. on stove top or if baking 30-35 min. Serves 10-12

Preheat oven to 375°

Ingredients:

4 tablespoons	olive oil
1 medium	onion, peeled and diced
3 stalks	celery, sliced
1 large	leek, sliced with greens
2 large	apples (red) or pears, diced
1 pound	focaccia stuffing or any bread stuffing
4 cups	chicken broth or turkey stock
1-1/2 cups	chestnuts, cooked, drained and chopped
1 cup	hazelnuts, walnuts or almonds, coarsely chopped
2 teaspoons	Herbes de Provençe

Sauté onion, celery and leek in a pan with oil until translucent. Remove from heat and place in a mixing bowl. Add apples or pears, then focaccia stuffing or other bread stuffing. Mix in broth and stir together. Make sure the stuffing is moistened with broth. Add chestnuts, nuts and Herbes de Provençe. Mix together.

To serve: As a side dish, spoon the stuffing into a casserole and bake at 375° until golden brown, approximately 30-35 minutes.

If desired, stuff the turkey. Make sure the inner temperature of the turkey and the stuffing is the same before stuffing is placed in turkey.

POLENTA

Polenta is corn meal. It is made of maize flour. It is a traditional Northern Italian dish and was Napoleon's favorite. It is one of the comfort foods. Great with pork, veal, lamb shanks or meatloaf.

Prep time: 20 min. Cook time: 40 min. Serves 6

Ingredients:

6 cups	chicken broth or any liquid
2 cups	yellow instant cornmeal
6 sprigs	basil leaves, chopped
salt and pepper	to taste

Boil water in a kettle. In an 8-quart Dutch oven, bring broth to a rolling boil. Transfer broth into a stainless steel or ovenproof bowl. Pour boiling water into the Dutch oven pan until it is 1/3 full. Continue heating water on medium heat. Place the bowl with broth, on top of a double-boiler. Slowly pour in cornmeal, whisking vigorously make sure there are no lumps. Reduce heat to a low simmer, cover bowl and stir occasionally.

Add basil, salt, pepper and whisk well. Cook on simmer for 40 minutes.

If serving this meal hot, just place on a large serving platter.

To Serve Cold As A Toast

1/2 cup	flour for dusting
1/3 cup	olive oil

Oil a 15x10x2 inch ovenproof baking dish. Spread polenta evenly.

To smooth, cut a piece of parchment paper the same size as the ovenproof pan. Press gently all over and smooth edges. Cover with same paper.

Let cool in refrigerator for a couple of hours. Cut into triangles. Flour the polenta pieces. Heat 1/3 cup of oil and brown pieces.

GORGONZOLA CELERY ROOT AND POTATO GRATIN

This bubbly au gratin is mouth watering. Celery root is also known as Celeriac. It is a variety of celery that has a large edible root. This recipe can be made ahead of time and baked the day it is served.

Prep time: 40 min. Cook time: 45 min. Serves 6

Preheat oven to 375°

Ingredients:

2 cloves	garlic, peeled and crushed
1 tablespoon	butter for gratin pan
2 pounds	Yukon gold potatoes, parboiled and peeled
1 pound	celery root, scrubbed
3 cups	water
3/4 teaspoon	salt
1/2 cup	heavy cream
2 teaspoons	Dijon mustard
1/4 teaspoon	ground black pepper
1/4 teaspoon	nutmeg
1 cup	Gorgonzola cheese, crumbled

Rub garlic inside of a 3 or 4-quart au gratin dish. Reserve garlic cloves. Butter au gratin dish evenly. Cut potatoes in half lengthwise, then slice them into 1/4 inch wide slices. Cut trimmings from celery root, and wash carefully to remove sand. Peel and cut celery root into quarters, then slice 1/4 inch wide. Place the trimmings and remaining garlic in a saucepan. Add 3 cups of water and salt. Add sliced celery root and sliced potatoes. Bring to a boil. Reduce heat and cook for 5 minutes until tender. Remove trimmings with tongs. Strain vegetables and reserve 1 cup of liquid. In a separate bowl, combine 1 cup of the reserved liquid with cream and mustard. Add strained vegetables, pepper, salt and nutmeg. Mix together. Pour into the buttered au gratin dish spreading evenly then sprinkle with crumbled Gorgonzola cheese. Bake 45 minutes until gratin is bubbly and browned on top.

TRI-COLOR PUREE

This is a very colorful and appetizing puree. Great for a buffet gathering. The Green Peas, Orange Glazed Carrots and Mashed Potatoes are a great marriage of tastes when eaten together. This recipe can be prepared ahead of time. Assemble several hours prior to serving. Cover with plastic wrap and refrigerate.

Prep time: 30 min. Cook time: 35 min. Serves 8

Ingredients:

Green Peas

4 cups	green peas, defrosted and drained
3 leaves	romaine lettuce
4 tablespoons	butter
1/4 cup	crème fraîche
salt and pepper	to taste

Blanch peas and lettuce leaves by immersing them in boiling water. Remove, drain and pour ice water over them to retain color. Place butter in food processor, add crème fraîche, salt and pepper. Add drained peas and lettuce. Process until a smooth puree. Remove and set aside.

Orange Glazed Carrots:

2 tablespoons	butter
1-1/2 pounds	small carrots, peeled and roughly diced
salt and pepper	to taste
1 tablespoon	fresh ginger, grated
1 medium	shallot, peeled and chopped
2 tablespoons	honey
1/2 cup	fresh squeezed orange juice

In a sauté pan, place butter and sauté carrots. Season with salt and pepper. Add ginger, shallot and cook over medium low heat, stirring occasionally. Add honey and orange juice. Cook until quite tender. Place in food processor and puree until smooth. Set aside.

Mashed Potatoes:

8 medium	Yukon gold potatoes, boiled and peeled
1 stick	butter
1/3 cup	milk or half and half
3 teaspoons	nutmeg
salt and pepper	to taste

Heat butter, milk or half and half, add nutmeg, salt and pepper in a saucepan. Mash potatoes with warm milk mixture. Set aside.

Garnish :

several	mint leaves
1 cup	cooked cranberries

Method to assemble when serving in a circular presentation:

Place pureed peas in a large pastry bag with a wide tip nozzle. Pipe peas in the center of the platter. Start in the middle of the platter and keep piping in a circle, leaving no spaces between circles, until all peas are used.

Fill another pastry bag with the carrot puree and pipe in a circle, leaving no spaces between circles. Start where the peas ended. Use all the carrot puree.

Repeat same process for mashed potatoes starting where carrots end. Use all of the potatoes

Garnish: Use mint leaves and cooked cranberries for garnish.

Optional serving suggestion:

Using a large platter, place the purees in a triangle meeting at a point in the center. Follow directions above for the garnish.

CORN SOUFFLE

This is a crowd pleaser. I remember making this recipe for hundreds of guests during my catering days. Gallons were stored in plastic containers and cooked the day before serving.

Prep time: 15 min. Cook time: 30 min. Serves 6

Preheat oven to 350°

Ingredients:

4 medium	eggs, separated
1-1/2 cups	heavy cream, milk or buttermilk
4 cups	corn, fresh or frozen, defrosted
1-1/2 cups	Bisquick
1 tablespoon	fresh thyme leaves
salt and pepper	to taste
1 teaspoon	sugar
2 cups	cheddar cheese, shredded
1 tablespoon	butter

Beat egg yolk and mix in cream, milk or buttermilk. If frozen, place corn in a colander to drain. Mix corn, Bisquick, thyme, salt, pepper and sugar into egg yolk mixture. Fold in grated cheddar cheese. Beat egg whites to a stiff peak. Gently fold beaten egg whites into corn mixture. Butter a 2 or 3-quart soufflé pan and pour in corn mixture. Place in pre-heated oven on the middle rack and bake for 30 minutes. Serve bubbly hot.

Artichoke Farm

SAUCES

AÏOLI

Aïoli is a typical sauce used in Provençe cooking. It can be done with garlic, mayonnaise and pepper. I tasted this sauce in Nice, France. It was a topping on bouillabaisse. I can still taste this! Serve on potatoes, fish and vegetables.

Prep time: 20 min. Makes 1 cup

Ingredients:

3 cloves	garlic, peeled and crushed
1 teaspoon	salt
2 large	eggs, yolks only
1 cup	olive oil
2 tablespoons	fresh lemon juice
1/2 teaspoon	pepper

Place crushed garlic in food processor bowl; add egg yolks and process. While processor is on, drizzle 1/2 cup olive oil, pouring it in a steady stream. Pour in lemon juice. Add pepper and process. While processor is on, slowly add remaining 1/2 cup of olive oil pouring in a steady stream. Process until mixture is thick to the consistency of mayonnaise.

MARINARA SAUCE

When making the Marinara Sauce double or triple the recipe and freeze in two cup containers. Great for using on several recipes. Add meat or sausage after it is defrosted.

Prep time: 30 min. Cook time: 1hr. Yields 1 quart

Ingredients:

2 tablespoons	olive oil
1 medium	onion peeled, chopped
4 cloves	garlic, peeled and crushed
1/4 cup	red wine
4 cups	pureed tomatoes
1(6 ounce)	can tomato paste
3 tablespoons	fresh oregano leaves, chopped
2 tablespoons	fresh thyme leaves, chopped
4 tablespoons	fresh basil leaves, chopped
salt and pepper	to taste

In a 6-quart pot, heat the olive oil over medium heat. Sauté onion and garlic until translucent. Stir in the wine. Add the puree and tomato paste, oregano, thyme and basil. Mix well.

Add salt and pepper to taste. Bring the sauce to a simmer, reduce the heat and cook over very low heat for at least 1 hour.

BÉCHAMEL SAUCE

The invention of Béchamel Sauce is attributed to the Marquis de Nointel and dedicated by a court chef to Mr. Béchamel. Many other sauces may be built from this basic sauce. Serve with chicken or veal. Can be used for casseroles and au gratin.

Prep time: 10 min. Cook time: 20 min. Makes 4 cups

Ingredients:

2 medium	bay leaves
4 cups	liquid (whole milk, broth)
4 tablespoons	butter
2 tablespoons	flour
1 teaspoon	nutmeg
salt	to taste
white pepper	to taste

Place bay leaves and liquid in a 2-quart saucepan. Heat until liquid is almost simmering.

Meanwhile melt the butter in another heavy 2-quart saucepan; then blend in flour with a wooden spoon or spatula. Cook over moderate heat until butter and flour foams and bubbles for two minutes. Color should be a buttery yellow.

Remove from heat and wait 30 seconds until roux has stopped bubbling. Pour the hot liquid into the roux. Add nutmeg, salt, and pepper. Beat vigorously with a wire whisk to make a perfectly smooth blend. Scrape with a rubber spatula all around and inside the corners of the pan to make sure roux has been absorbed by the liquid. Beat again for a few seconds.

Set saucepan over moderate heat and bring to a slow boil, stirring slowly taking a second to circulate the wire whisk. Simmer slowly for two minutes.

If you do not use the sauce immediately: clean side of pan with a rubber spatula; lay a piece of plastic wrap on top to prevent a crust; or take a small piece of butter and drop it on top of sauce and spread it over the top of the sauce with the back of a spoon.

WHITE SAUCE

This is my own version of a simple and easy sauce. The sauce is excellent for au gratin and casseroles. Great as a base for meatballs

Prep time: 10 min. Makes 3 cups

Ingredients:

8 ounces	cream cheese
1 cup	whipping cream, milk, or low-fat milk
1 cup	crumbled feta cheese
salt	to taste
white pepper	to taste

Use a blender or food processor. Blend ingredients until smooth, and add salt and pepper to taste.

MUSHROOM DILL MIXTURE

This sauce is very good when used with fish, meat, pasta or vegetable. Use as a base for casseroles and au gratin.

Prep time: 10 min. Cook time: 10 min. Makes 4 cups

Ingredients:

2 tablespoons	butter or olive oil
1 pound	mushroom, sliced
1 bunch	green onions (scallions), sliced
1/4 cup	cognac
1/2 ounce	fresh dill, chopped
salt and pepper	to taste
3 cups	White Sauce, see recipe

Melt butter or olive oil. Add mushrooms, onions, cognac and sauté until juices evaporate. Add dill, salt and pepper. Combine the White Sauce recipe with the mixture.

WALNUT SAUCE

This sauce is excellent as a topping on baked potato. It can also be used as a dip. It is wonderful when served with poultry and meat.

Prep time: 10 min. Makes 2-1/2 cups

Ingredients:

1 pound	walnuts, finely chopped
2 tablespoons	Panko breadcrumbs
1 roll	soaked in water, squeezed
2 tablespoons	olive oil
2 tablespoons	molasses
2 tablespoons	lemon juice
1/2 teaspoon	red-hot chili sauce
1 teaspoon	caraway seeds
1 teaspoon	salt
water	as needed

Using a food processor, blend all the above ingredients well. Add a little water for desired consistency. Continue blending until sauce becomes smooth and thick.

YOGURT PINE NUTS SAUCE

This sauce is great with Kibbee Croquettes. Sauce is also wonderful when used as a topping for steamed vegetables.

Prep time: 8 min. Makes 1-1/2 cups

Ingredients:

1 tablespoon	olive oil
4 tablespoons	pine nuts
1 cup	yogurt (plain or low fat)
1 clove	garlic, peeled and crushed
1 tablespoon	lemon juice
20 medium	mint leaves

Place olive oil in a sauté pan. Sauté pine nuts until light brown.

In a food processor, place pine nuts, yogurt, crushed garlic, lemon juice, mint leaves and process together for just 2 seconds. Remove and place in serving bowl.

SAUCE VERTE

Sauce Verte in French means green sauce. Serve with salmon or other fish. Very good as a dip for shrimp.

Prep time: 10 min. Makes 2 cups

Ingredients:

1/2 bunch	fresh spinach, stems removed, washed and chopped
2 tablespoons	fresh parsley, stems removed, washed and chopped
1 tablespoon	dill weed or 2 tablespoons fresh dill
1 cup	mayonnaise
2 tablespoons	crème fraîche or yogurt

Using a food processor or blender, mix all ingredients until smooth; chill until ready to serve.

SKORDALIA
POTATO GARLIC PUREE

This is a rustic Greek sauce. Sauce is also used in Middle Eastern cooking as a topping on grilled chicken.

Prep time: 20 min. Cook time: 30–45 min. Makes 4 cups

Ingredients:

2 pounds	potatoes, cooked and peeled
8 cloves	garlic, peeled and crushed
1 cup	olive oil
1/2 cup	wine vinegar
1/2 tablespoon	salt
white pepper	to taste

Puree potatoes with a masher or ricer. Place in a bowl; add crushed garlic, olive oil, wine vinegar, salt and pepper. Mix together.

ROMESCO SAUCE

This sauce is of Spanish origin. It is incredible on grilled meats and fish. Sauce can be used as a dip or on bruschetta.

Prep time: 30 min. Makes 3 cups

Ingredients:

4 ounces	blanched almonds or raw pistachio nuts
3/4 cup	fresh basil leaves
5 slices	Italian or French bread, cut into half inch pieces
1 (6 ounce)	jar, roasted red pepper, rinsed and drained
3 ounces	chicken broth
2 cloves	garlic, peeled and crushed
2 tablespoons	tomato paste
1 tablespoon	paprika
1 pinch	cayenne pepper
1 tablespoon	brandy
1/4 cup	red wine vinegar
1 medium	lemon, juiced
1 cup	extra virgin olive oil

Place nuts in food processor bowl or blender; process until finely chopped. Add basil and process. Add bread and process until consistency of medium crumbs. While processor is running, drizzle broth into the nut and crumb mixture. Add remaining ingredients except oil and process until smooth. While processor is running, drizzle the olive oil into mixture. If consistency is too thick, add a little broth or lemon juice.

MANGO GINGER SAUCE

During the summer you can use peaches, apricots or nectarines. This is best served with mango sorbet or ice cream and brownies. This is a good recipe to freeze.

Prep time: 10 min. Makes 1 cup

Ingredients:

1 tablespoon	fresh ginger, grated
1/2 cup	fresh orange juice
1-1/2 tablespoons	fresh mango, chopped
3 tablespoons	fresh lime juice
3 tablespoons	honey

Place all ingredients in the food processor or blender. Puree until blended.

RASPBERRY COULIS

A coulis is made when fruit is pureed to a very thin consistency. This raspberry coulis is a great topping for dessert. I usually use this coulis on poached pears, chocolate mousse, sorbet and bundt cake.

Prep time: 10 min. Makes 4-1/2 cups

Ingredients:

2 pints (1 quart)	fresh raspberries
1/4 cup	sugar
1/3 cup	fresh orange juice
1 tablespoon	raspberry flavored liqueur (Framboise)

Place ingredients in food processor or blender; process until pureed. Strain sauce.

STRAWBERRIES IN LEMON BALSAMIC SAUCE

Instead of strawberries, try using blueberries or raspberries. Serve with ice cream or as a topping for cake or fruits.

Prep time: 10 min. Makes 2-1/2 cups

Ingredients:

1/4 cup	lemon juice
2 tablespoons	sugar
1 tablespoon	balsamic vinegar
2 cups	strawberries, hulled and quartered

Place all ingredients into food processor. Puree until blended.

MASCARPONE ALMOND SAUCE

This sauce is wonderful when used as a topping on ice cream, bundt cake, chocolate mousse and poached fruits.

Prep time: 10 min. Makes 1 cup

Ingredients:

8 ounces	mascarpone
1/2 teaspoon	almond extract
1/4 cup	honey

Mix ingredients together.

DESSERTS

BEST BAKLAVA

Baklava has many alluring variations. Sometimes almonds or walnuts are used exclusively or a combination of both can be used. My version is a combination of three types of nuts. To achieve a crisp pastry it is essential to pour the cooled syrup over hot pastry or pour hot syrup over cooled pastry. The Greek version of syrup is made of honey, while the Middle Eastern version is made with sugar syrup. I like to add lemon and orange water. Orange or rose water can be purchased in Middle Eastern specialty stores.

Prep time: 1 hr. Cook time: 30-40 min. Makes 66 pieces

Preheat oven to 350°

Ingredients:

Syrup:

2 cups	granulated sugar
3/4 cups	water
2 tablespoons	lemon juice
2 tablespoons	orange or rose water

Filling:

1-3/4 cup	chopped walnuts
1-3/4 cup	unsalted almonds
2 cups	unsalted raw pistachio nuts
3/4 cup	granulated sugar
1 tablespoon	cinnamon

Phyllo:

1 pound	phyllo package
3/4 pound	butter, clarified

Keep phyllo package in refrigerator until ready to use.

To make syrup: Place sugar and water in a heavy saucepan. Stir over medium heat until sugar has dissolved. Add lemon juice, orange or rose water, stir. Bring the syrup to a boil. Keep simmering on medium heat for 15 minutes. Do not stir after it begins to boil. Remove from heat and let cool.

To make filling: Place nuts in the food processor bowl. Using a steel blade finely chop nuts. Place the chopped nuts in a mixing bowl, add cinnamon, sugar and mix all together. Divide filling into 3 equal parts.

To clarify butter: Place 1 pound butter in a saucepan, melt over low heat. Skim froth from top. Let butter stand for a minute to allow solids to settle. Pour or spoon off the oiled butter into a container, leaving milk solids in the pan. Use clarified butter while warm.

To assemble Baklava: Butter the base and sides of a 15x10x2 oven proof baking dish. Place a damp cloth on a cutting board or counter, top with plastic wrap. Unfold phyllo dough, place on top of plastic wrap. Cover with a dry towel and top with damp one. Divide phyllo sheets into 4, place a book mark between the 4 sections. You will have 4 stacks. A 1-pound package of phyllo has approximately 20 to 24 sheets.

Place a sheet of phyllo in the buttered baking dish. Butter the top of the sheet. If needed fold the edges to fit the dish. Repeat same until 5 sheets have been used. Sprinkle one third of nut filling on buttered phyllo. Butter one sheet from the second stack. Place the buttered side of phyllo down on top of filling. Press gently. Repeat same procedure until all sheets and filling have been used. Carefully butter the top sheet. Cut baklava with a sharp knife into diamond shapes. Cut diagonal lines 1-1/2 inches apart, then vertical lines. Make sure you cut all the way down. Butter again. Spray lightly with water to prevent top layers from curling upwards.

To bake: Place Baklava on center shelf of preheated oven. Bake for 30-35 minutes until brown. Remove from heat. Immediately pour cooled syrup over hot baklava, and make sure the syrup covers all the pieces. Recut baklava pieces with tip of a sharp knife. Let cool before removing pieces to a serving platter.

Baklava can be frozen after being cooked. To defrost, leave at room temperature.

INDIVIDUAL TIRAMISU

Tiramisu means pick me up. Eating this dessert definitely gives you a lift. This recipe is quite easy to make as well as delicious. I recommend preparing this Tiramisu ahead of time. It has become a very popular dessert in the US. My greatest memory was when I made hundreds of trays of Tiramisu for 1,500 people. Use the best cocoa you can find. I like the Dutch Cocoa.

Prep time: 30 min. Chill: 2 hrs. Serves 6

Ingredients:

8 ounces	mascarpone cheese
2 tablespoons	confectioners' sugar
1/2 cup	crème fraîche
2 tablespoons	cherry brandy
1 cup	strong coffee or espresso
4 tablespoons	coffee liqueur
12 ladyfingers	broken into thirds
1/4 cup	powdered cocoa
2 tablespoons	milk chocolate, grated

In a bowl mix mascarpone cheese with confectioners' sugar, crème fraîche and cherry brandy. Set aside.

Mix coffee and coffee liqueur in a bowl. Lightly dip broken ladyfingers into the coffee/coffee liqueur mixture. Place the dipped pieces of ladyfingers in the bottom of six martini glasses. Spoon on a layer of mascarpone mixture, and sprinkle each with cocoa and grated chocolate. Repeat the layers with the remaining three pieces of ladyfingers, coffee/coffee liqueur, mascarpone mixture, cocoa and chocolate. Cover and chill for 2 hours prior to serving.

CLAFOUTI LIMOUSIN

The classical definition of Clafouti is a flan. It is a thick crêpe baked in the oven with cherries. Limousin is a region of France. This is a rustic dessert shared at the family table. Clafouti is simple, yet hearty and a fulfilling end to a meal. It is a well-known dessert and quite popular in Provençe where there are ample berries, especially during the cherry season. I usually make this dessert when the fruits, such as pears, apricots, apples and peaches, are over ripe. In the winter on a cold day, I will use frozen berries.

Prep time: 10 min. Cook time: 35 min. Serves 6

Preheat oven to 425°

Ingredients:

2 pounds	berries, fresh <u>or</u> frozen
3 tablespoons	kirsch (cherry liqueur)
2/3 cup	granulated sugar
3 large	eggs
1 cup	heavy cream
2 tablespoons	butter for 10-1/2 inch porcelain baking pan

Topping:

1/2 cup	confectioners' sugar
8 ounces	crème fraîche
6 teaspoons	marmalade
1 cup	juice from cooked berries

If frozen berries are used, defrost, drain. When fresh berries are used, wash and gently pat dry with paper towel. Place berries in an oven proof dish.

Toss berries with 2 tablespoons sugar and 1 tablespoon kirsch. Place berries in oven proof dish and bake for 10 minutes until fruit is hot and steaming. Remove from oven. Drain cooked berries and save 1 cup of juice to flavor the baked Clafouti. Lower temperature of oven to 350°.

In a mixer, whisk eggs until frothy. Add remaining sugar and whisk. Combine cream until frothy, add remaining sugar and whisk. Combine cream, and 2 tablespoons kirsch. Beat until well blended and set aside. Butter a 10-1/2 inch round porcelain baking pan.

Transfer the drained berries to the porcelain baking pan and arrange in a single layer, carefully pour half of the batter on top of the berries.

Place on the center rack of the oven and bake for 5 minutes. Remove from oven. Add the remaining batter. This avoids spilling over on to the bottom of the oven. Continue to bake for 35 minutes. Remove from oven.

Preheat oven broiler. Place Clafouti under the broiler to brown the top. Remove and set aside.

To serve: May be served either hot or at room temperature. Sprinkle with confectioners' sugar and top with crème fraîche. Spoon marmalade on top and drizzle with berry cooking juices.

Poached Pears in Phyllo Nests, see recipe on page 146-147.

POACHED PEARS IN PHYLLO NESTS

Pears have been very popular with gourmands for a long time. Pears are at their best when in season which is September-October. The Romans cultivated pears. Pears are one of my favorite fruits. They are majestically beautiful and easily digested. The flesh contains a large number of mineral salts. Pears are an excellent dessert. The color of these poached pears is red. This dessert can be made without the phyllo nests if desired.

Prep time: 15 min. Cook time: 45 min. Serves 3

Preheat oven to 350°

Ingredients:

Poaching Liquid:

2 cups	granulated sugar
4 cups	red wine (Cabernet Sauvignon or Merlot)
2 cups	cranberry juice
1 stick	vanilla bean
3 medium	pears, with stems, peeled

For the Phyllo Nests:

3 sheets	phyllo dough
2 ounces	melted butter

Nut Mixture:

2 tablespoons	white raisins
2 tablespoons	pistachio nuts, chopped
2 tablespoons	walnuts, chopped
5 large	dates, pitted and chopped
1 tablespoon	granulated sugar
2 tablespoons	brandy or cognac

Sauce:

Reduced	poaching liquid
4 tablespoons	grape jelly

Garnish: zested lemon peel

In a large saucepan, place sugar, wine, cranberry juice and vanilla bean. Bring to a boil, reduce to simmering. Peel pears starting one inch from top. Core bottom of pears with melon baller. Cut bottom straight for balance. Place pears in poaching liquid, cook over medium heat for 15 minutes. Remove from heat and let cool in the liquid.

To make phyllo nests: Cut each phyllo sheet into fourths and brush with butter. Press the four pieces into a 5-inch tart mold, or muffin pan and decoratively fold edges. Repeat the procedure with remaining phyllo pieces. Place molds on parchment lined sheet pan. Bake for 10 minutes or until golden brown. Remove from oven set aside to cool.

To make the nut mixture: Place raisins, nuts, dates, sugar, brandy or cognac in a food processor bowl, process together until finely chopped.

Cook sauce on low heat until reduced. Add grape jelly.

To serve: Place to 2 tablespoons of the sauce on each plate and set phyllo nests beside it. Put a pear inside the nest, and spoon nut mixture on an unused portion of the plate. Garnish with zest of lemon peel.

MARBLED BROWNIES

I have taken Marbled Brownies on several picnics. One in particular was when I took a group of my students to Amador County on a field trip and had a "Food Pairing with Wines" class. The brownies were served with an accompaniment of Vintage Port and Orange Muscat. It was incredibly delicious together.

Prep time: 35 min. Cook time: 35 min. Makes 15 pieces

Preheat oven to 350°

Ingredients:

12 ounces	German sweet chocolate
6 tablespoons	butter
3 large	eggs, beaten
1 cup	granulated sugar
1/2 teaspoon	baking powder
1/4 teaspoon	salt
1/2 cup plus	1 tablespoon flour
1/2 cup	pistachio nuts, chopped
1-1/2 teaspoons	vanilla
1 teaspoon	almond extract
8 ounces	cream cheese

Melt chocolate with 3 tablespoons of butter, let cool. Beat 2 eggs, add 3/4 cup sugar, and beat until thick. Add baking powder, salt and flour. Blend in cooled chocolate and pistachio nuts. Add 1 teaspoon vanilla, 1/2 teaspoon almond extract, set aside.

Beat 3 tablespoons butter with cream cheese until it softens. Add 1/4 cup sugar, the remaining egg, 1 tablespoon flour, 1/2 teaspoon vanilla and 1/2 teaspoon almond extract. Mix together well.

In a greased 8x8 inch square pan, spread about half the chocolate batter. Spread all of the cheese batter on top covering evenly.

Drop remaining half chocolate batter in globs over the top of the cheese batter. Zigzag with a spatula through the batter to marble. Bake in preheated oven until top springs back. Check at approximately 30 minutes. The brownies should be soft and not overcooked.

Let cool. If needed, refrigerate prior to cutting the slices. Slice with a plastic knife.

Best Baklava, see recipe on page140-141.

Sensually Delicious Chocolate Mousse, see recipe on page150.

SENSUALLY DELICIOUS CHOCOLATE MOUSSE

This chocolate mousse is guaranteed to steal your heart. I love savoring every spoonful of this mousse. Men in particular drool just mentioning this mousse. Freeze leftovers. Serve the mousse in chocolate cups, which are available in gourmet stores.

Prep time: 35 min. Serves 10

Ingredients:

8 ounces	semisweet imported chocolate, cut in pieces
5 large	eggs, separated
1-1/2 sticks	unsalted sweet butter
1/2 cup	Irish cream liqueur
1/8 teaspoon	cream of tartar
1 pint	heavy whipping cream
2 tablespoons	confectioners' sugar
6 ounces	semisweet mini chocolate chips

Cut chocolate into little pieces. Melt chocolate in a double boiler until all pieces are melted. Make sure no steam escapes, otherwise chocolate will separate or curdle. Another option is to microwave for 40 seconds, remove and stir.

Place egg yolks in a separate bowl and beat over a double boiler to heat. Place egg whites in another bowl. Make sure the egg white bowl is well washed, dried, rubbed with salt, then wiped with a paper towel.

Cut butter into small pieces and place in food processor bowl along with egg yolks. Beat in egg yolks with butter. Add Irish cream liqueur to the egg/butter mixture and mix well.

Beat egg whites with cream of tartar until stiff. Gently fold melted chocolate into egg whites.

Whip heavy cream in another chilled bowl. Gradually add the confectioners' sugar and continue whipping until stiff.

Fold egg white/chocolate mixture into the egg yolk/butter/Irish cream liqueur mixture.

Fold in whipping cream. Sprinkle with mini chocolate chips and fold. Pour into individual glasses, or into a bowl. Refrigerate overnight or for several hours.

AUTUMN BUNDT CAKE

Autumn Bundt Cake is also known as ABC cake. It is great to make it for Thanksgiving or Christmas. The banana squash is available in supermarkets in the fall. Leftover Halloween pumpkin may be used instead of the banana squash. The banana squash is easier to grate than raw pumpkin. If you decide to substitute pumpkin, make sure you parboil it first.

Prep time: 30 - 40 min. Cook time: 55 min. Serves 10-12

Preheat oven to 325°

Ingredients:

2 cups	unbleached all purpose flour
2 teaspoons	double acting baking powder
2 teaspoons	baking soda
1 teaspoon	salt
1/4 teaspoon	ginger, freshly grated
1/4 teaspoon	ground mace
1 tablespoon	cinnamon
7 large	dried prunes, pitted
3/4 cup	pecans
3 cups	banana squash or Halloween pumpkin, peeled and grated
4 large	eggs
2 cups	granulated sugar
1-1/2 cups	oil
3/4 cup	dried cherries

Garnish:

orange	food coloring
4 ounces	white chocolate

Adjust oven rack to the middle level.

Put the flour, baking powder, baking soda, salt and spices in the food processor bowl with the steel blade and process for about 2 minutes. Leave 1 tablespoon of the mixture in the food processor bowl; remove the rest to another bowl.

Put the prunes in the food processor bowl and process for 10 seconds until finely chopped. Add the nuts and process for 5 seconds. Transfer the mixture to a larger mixing bowl.

Add grated banana squash to the prune mixture and set aside.

Put the eggs and sugar in the food processor and process for one minute, or until the mixture is thick and light colored. With the machine running, pour the oil through the feed tube and process for one full minute, or until the mixture is fluffy, stopping once to scrape down the sides of the bowl. Add the dry ingredients and combine by turning the machine on and off 4 or 5 times, or only until the flour just disappears. Do not over process.

Pour mixture and combine into the banana squash and prune mixture. Add the dried cherries. Mix together with a spatula.

Pour the batter into a greased and floured 12-cup bundt pan and smooth the top with a spatula. Bake in a preheated oven for 55 minutes or until a toothpick inserted in the center comes out clean. Allow the cake to cool in the pan for 10 minutes. Invert onto a wire rack. Let the cake cool completely. Remove bundt pan.

Melt white chocolate adding a drop of orange food coloring. Drizzle on top of cake.

Autumn Bundt Cake

Orange Panna Cotta – Macerated Orange Sauce, see recipe on page 154.

ORANGE PANNA COTTA

Panna Cotta is an Italian cooked-molded cream dessert. Panna Cotta means cooked cream in Italian. It is a sublime dessert and quite easy to make. The presentation is quite impressive when the macerated orange sauce is poured on top of the Panna Cotta.

Prep time: 10 min. Cook time: 20 min. Serves 4 to 6

Ingredients:

1/2 cup	orange juice
2 packages	unflavored gelatin
4 cups	heavy cream or milk
1 cup	confectioners' sugar
2 teaspoons	orange liqueur
1/4 teaspoon	salt
1 large	orange, zested
1 cup	crème fraîche

Place orange juice in a small bowl. Sprinkle the unflavored gelatin in the bowl. Set for 10 minutes to soften gelatin. In a large 3-quart saucepan combine heavy cream, sugar, orange liqueur, 1/4 teaspoon salt and orange zest. Heat over medium heat. Do not let it boil. Stir in orange gelatin mixture. Remove from heat. Whisk together until gelatin is dissolved. Let mixture cool at room temperature for 5 minutes.

Gently whisk the crème fraîche and gradually add to Panna Cotta mixture a little at a time until smooth. Pour into a bowl and let cool in the refrigerator. Spray and line a 5-cup mold with plastic wrap. Pour the Orange Panna Cotta into the mold. Refrigerate for at least 4 hours. Unmold onto dessert plate and serve with Macerated Orange Sauce.

To serve: Place individually in wine or martini glasses.

MACERATED ORANGE SAUCE

The term macerated is commonly used for fruits. The act of macerating is when fruits are placed into a container that has a sauce, or some form of liquid where the fruits can absorb the flavors of the sauce in which they are placed.

Prep time: 15 min. Macerating time: 2 hrs. Serves 6

Ingredients:

2 medium	oranges zested, sliced in rings
3 tablespoons	granulated sugar
3 tablespoons	orange liqueur

Wash oranges, using the zester make strips 1/2 inch apart starting from top of the orange to the bottom of orange. Save zest for garnishing.

In a large platter or bowl place a layer of sliced oranges. Drizzle with some orange liqueur and sprinkle some sugar. Repeat same until all orange slices are used. Pour remaining orange liqueur and sugar on top. Let macerate for at least 2 hours.

To serve: Top Panna Cotta with this Macerated Orange Sauce.

DECIDEDLY DELICIOUS CHOCOLATE BREAD PUDDING

This recipe is ideal for leftover bread. It is so good on a cold evening. This is one of the best comfort foods to enjoy. So quick and easy to make. Everyone who tastes it, seems to fall in love with this recipe. The Chocolate Bread Pudding can be assembled ahead and baked before serving or baked ahead and reheated in the microwave for a short time.

Prep time: 30 min. Cook time: 50 min. Serves 8

Preheat oven to 350°

Ingredients:

6 cups	French or whole-wheat bread, cut into 1 inch cubes
1-1/2 cups	heavy cream or low-fat milk.
1 cup	dried cranberries
1/4 cup	cognac or brandy
2 ounces	bittersweet chocolate
1 ounce	unsweetened chocolate
3 large	eggs, separated
3 ounces	sweet butter, at room temperature
1/3 cup	granulated sugar
1/2 cup	raw pistachio nuts

In a bowl, place bread cubes and cream. Soak for at least 30 minutes.

Place cranberries in cognac and soak for at least 10 minutes.

Cut chocolate in small pieces and place on top of a double boiler until melted. Keep warm.

Cream together butter, sugar and egg yolks in a bowl until blended. Add soaked bread cubes, pistachio nuts, cranberries and melted chocolate. Mix well.

Beat egg whites to soft peaks. Fold egg whites into chocolate mixture.

Lightly butter the inside of a 3-quart casserole or soufflé pan. Pour in the chocolate bread pudding batter. Place casserole in a roasting pan. Set the pan in the oven. Carefully pour enough hot water to come at least halfway up the sides of a roasting pan.

Bake for 40 to 50 minutes. Take out of the oven and remove the casserole from the water bath and allow to cool for 10 minutes.

To serve: Top with Mascarpone Almond Sauce or vanilla ice cream.

PÊCHES FARCIES A LA PISTACHE
STUFFED PEACHES WITH PISTACHIO NUTS

The peach tree originated in Persia. It is one of the best and most attractive of fruits. Yellow peaches mature later than the white-fleshed variety. They make a good preserving fruit. In Northern California we have an abundance of fabulous looking orchards with incredible tastes, flavors and colors. The season for peaches in Northern California is from May to August. This peach dessert is so easy to make especially when the peaches are quite ripe.

Prep time: 20 min. Cook time: 5 min. Makes 14 halves

Ingredients:

7 large	yellow ripe fresh peaches, washed and pit removed
1/2 medium	lemon
2 medium	biscotti, hazelnut chocolate or plain
2 tablespoons	marzipan
1 tablespoon	peach liqueur
2 tablespoons	pistachio nuts
2 tablespoons	granulated sugar

Garnish:

14 medium	mint leaves
8 ounces	crème fraîche
2 teaspoons	pistachio nuts, chopped

In a food processor bowl, place biscotti, marzipan, peach liqueur and pistachio nuts (save some for garnish) and process together until coarsely chopped.

Cut peaches in half and rub with lemon. Place 1-1/2 teaspoons of the biscotti mixture in pit cavity of each half peach, press down and shape to resemble a pit. Sprinkle with sugar, and place under the broiler for 5 minutes until the top becomes lightly brown. Remove and place on serving platter.

To serve: Place a teaspoon of crème fraîche in the center of the filling, garnish with a mint leaf, and sprinkle with chopped pistachio nuts.

Northern California Peaches

SEASONAL GRILLED FRUIT KEBAB

People usually are surprised when mentioning the Seasonal Grilled Fruit Kebab. When the fruits are grilled, the intense delicious flavor in them is emphasized. It is quite important to soak the bamboo skewers prior to grilling in order to avoid burning the skewers. The macerating of the fruits helps bring out the flavors as well as make them tender. Fruits that are in season, may be used as substitutes for the ones in this recipe. Long bamboo skewers should be soaked in water overnight prior to being used.

Prep time: 30 min. Cook time: 6 min. Macerating time: 2-3 hrs. Serves 6

Ingredients:

4 large	apricots, cut in half, pit removed
2 large	peaches, cut in half, pit removed
1 large	apple, unpeeled, cut into quarters
1 large	orange, unpeeled, cut into quarters
1/2 medium	pineapple, unpeeled cut into 1 inch cubes

Macerating Mixture:

1 cup	honey
1/2 cup	rum
1 teaspoon	cinnamon

Mix macerating ingredients together. If needed heat honey and rum in a saucepan, add cinnamon. Place all cut fruits in the macerating mixture and let soak for at least 2 or 3 hours. Place a piece of each fruit on a skewer that has been soaked in water overnight. Grill with skin down for 6 minutes. Remove and place on serving platter. Drizzle remaining macerating mixture while fruits are hot.

See photo on page 160

MILLE-FEUILLE FIG NAPOLEON

Mille-Feuille is a pastry that is quite popular in France. It is made by arranging several layers of flaky pastry one on top of another with a filling in between. My version of this classical dessert is quite simple and fast. Use phyllo dough rather than puff pastry. If you choose to make your own custard you can. I prefer to get a package of imported English dessert mix custard and doctor it. This particular custard style pudding is available in most supermarkets in the gelatin section. Raspberries and blackberries may be used in place of figs. This recipe can be prepared ahead by baking the phyllo sheets, soaking the raisins and chopping the pistachio nuts the day before. Make the custard a couple of hours prior to serving.

Prep time: 30 min. Cook time: 15-20 min. Makes 8 pieces

Preheat oven to 350°

Ingredients:

Custard:

2 tablespoons	orange liqueur
1/2 cup	dark raisins
1/2 cup	pistachio nuts, chopped
2 packages	(sachets) imported English dessert custard style pudding
1/4 cup	granulated sugar
3 cups	milk or half and half
1 teaspoon	vanilla paste, or 2 sticks of vanilla beans

Mille-Feuille:

8 tablespoons	butter, clarified
6 sheets	phyllo dough
4 tablespoons	granulated sugar

Filling:

8 large	black or white figs, gently washed and dried, unpeeled and sliced vertically or 1 pint each of raspberries and blackberries

Garnish:

8 large	black or white figs, cut in half for garnishing or
1/2 pint	berries instead of figs
8 leaves	mint
1 cup	confectioners' sugar

Place orange liqueur in a bowl. Add raisins and chopped pistachio nuts. Soak for 10 minutes. In a saucepan, stir in custard pudding and sugar. Gradually whisk in milk until smooth. Add vanilla bean or paste, set directly over medium heat and stir slowly with a wooden spoon reaching all over bottom and sides of pan. Continue stirring until the custard is smooth and has thickened. Remove from heat and place in an 8-inch ovenproof dish. Mix in soaked raisins and chopped pistachio nuts, cover with plastic wrap and let cool at room temperature or refrigerate.

Clarify butter. Remove 6 sheets of phyllo from package. Wrap unused portion and return to package and seal well. Place the 6 phyllo sheets on top of parchment paper. Cover with plastic wrap, then with a moistened dishtowel. Place first phyllo sheet on cutting board, butter and sprinkle it with sugar. Repeat same process several times until 6 sheets have been used.

Butter a baking sheet. Make a pattern by cutting a cardboard piece 2x3-1/4 inches. Place the 2 inch measurement of the pattern on the length side of the phyllo sheets and the 3-1/4 inch measurement on the width part of the phyllo sheet. Cut the pattern all the way through the 6 sheets. Place the cut pieces on a buttered baking sheet. Bake for 10 minutes until light brown.

To assemble: Place 2 pieces of the baked 2x3-1/4 phyllo on a platter and spoon 2 tablespoons of custard mixture. Cover the layer of custard with slices of fig, top with another 2 pieces of phyllo. Repeat the process until finished. Sprinkle with confectioners' sugar, garnish with 2 halves of fig and a mint leaf. Or you may use the berries instead of figs.

Mille-Feuille Fig Napoleon and Seasonal Grilled Fruit Kabobs, see recipes on pages 158-160.

GRILLING MENU

Agave Salmon, see recipe on page 87; Medley Grilled Vegetables, see recipe on page 124; Mediterranean Grilled Chicken, see recipe on page 163.

ALL ABOUT GRILLING

Grilling is universal. People all around the world cook over open fire. This is how cooking began and it stood the test of time. Today it is the favorite method of cooking.

Global Grilling. Every country has its own grilling dishes. In Peru they have Anticuchos, spicy kebabs made with beef heart. Mexico, has Barbacoa, pit roasted spiced marinated lamb. Tuscany, Bistecca alla Florentina, olive oil marinated steak. Yugoslavia, Cevapcici, round meat patties. France, Grillade, grilled steaks or chops. Middle East, Kefta, ground kebabs. Morocco, Mechoui, spit roasted lamb, Greece, Souvlaki, lamb shish kebab. Italy, Spiedini, Italian shish kebab.

Grilling is fun specially when family and friends gather around the fire.

The incredible smell of the grilled food is mouth watering and quite appetizing. Grilling is easy, it does not need much preparation, just organization. It eliminates all the mess in the kitchen.

Types of Grills. Charcoal grills, gas grills, ridged cast iron grill pans, broilers. Charcoal grills should light up 35-40 minutes to preheat before starting to grill. Gas grills 12-15 minutes to preheat the lava rocks. For ridged cast iron pans, set over a medium high heat 4 minutes before grilling. For broilers, allow 8-10 minutes to preheat an electric broiler and 5 minutes for a gas broiler.

Tools Needed for Grilling. Long handled tongs. Long metal spatula. Grill rack. Natural bristle basting brush. Instant read thermometer. Stiff wire brush for cleaning grill. Serving platters.

Tips on grilling. Brush the grill rack with a stiff wire brush while it is still hot, to loosen any charred remains. Recommend doing this after you finish grilling.

Testing the grill is important. Splash a few drops of water on the surface; when it sizzles and evaporates it is ready.

Do not poke, prod or attempt to turn the food during the first minute of grilling. Never overcrowd the food on the rack. Do not wander off.

Never use the same container the food has been marinated in. If the marinade is being used make sure you boil it first prior to serving.

The exact time is difficult to predict. Therefore it is important to test the food while it is grilling. For fish test using a fork to prod gently when the flesh is firm and is beginning to flake. For chicken remove a piece and place on a cutting board, make a cut into the meat with a sharp knife. The flesh should be opaque throughout with no trace of pink at the bone.

MEDITERRANEAN GRILLED CHICKEN

When marinating raw chicken, make sure the cooked chicken is not put in the same container unless properly washed. If the marinade is to be used later, make sure it is cooked by boiling the sauce. If using chicken breasts or boneless, skinless chicken, hold the lemon juice until the breasts are cooked. Add the lemon juice to the reserved marinade at the end before heating and pour on top. Lemon tends to toughen the breasts. Cook the chicken breasts for 15 minutes on each side. Cook boneless, skinless chicken for only 8 minutes on each side.

Prep time: 1hr. 20 min. Cook time: 24 min. Serves 6

Ingredients:

Herbes Marinade:

4 cloves	garlic, peeled and crushed
1/2 cup	fresh lemon juice
1 teaspoon	allspice or nutmeg
1 teaspoon	salt
1/2 teaspoon	pepper
1 cup	olive oil
4 sprigs	fresh oregano, leaves only
4 sprigs	fresh thyme, leaves only
4 sprigs	basil, leaves only

Chicken:

3 pounds	chicken drumsticks, thighs or both.

In a food processor bowl, place all ingredients for marinade; process until well blended.

Wash and dry chicken pieces. With scissors or knife, slit the top of the drums and thighs.

In a single layer, with slit side down, place drumsticks and thighs in a shallow pan. Pour some of the marinade over the chicken, save the rest for later. Toss the chicken pieces with marinade. Let marinate for at least 1 hour.

Preheat the grill on high for 5 minutes, then reduce to medium heat. Place marinated chicken pieces with slit side down on the grill. Cook on one side for 12 minutes turn and cook for another 12 minutes.

Heat reserved marinade in a saucepan, and bring to boil. Place grilled chicken on a serving platter. Pour Herbes Marinade on top and serve.

See photo on pate 161

Jeanette Grilling

Chad Grilling

Group Toasting

Group Party

Table Setting

GAZPACHO ANDALUSIA

This recipe is great for hot summer days, picnics or a large group party. I tasted the best Gazpacho when I lived in Madrid. Prior to food processors and canned tomatoes, the gazpacho was done by squeezing fresh tomatoes. I still can taste this delicious recipe sipping it on a veranda in Madrid. I watched how they did it. This started my addiction to Gazpacho.

Prep time: 30 min. Makes 15 8-ounce cups

Ingredients:

2 medium	yellow peppers, seeded and coarsely chopped
2 medium	red peppers, seeded and coarsely chopped
2 medium	cucumbers, peeled and chopped into chunks
2 medium	onions, peeled and coarsely chopped
5 cloves	garlic, peeled and chopped
8 medium	ripe tomatoes, coarsely chopped
4 cups	tomato juice
1/2 cup	balsamic vinegar
3 medium	limes, juiced
1 tablespoon	fresh thyme
1/2 cup	extra virgin olive oil
2 teaspoons	Tabasco sauce (optional)
4 slices	plain Italian bread
salt and pepper	to taste

Garnish:

1 medium	yellow pepper, seeded and finely diced
1 small	red onion, finely diced
1 cup	croutons, cut into small pieces

Using a food processor or blender, combine all ingredients and process or blend according to desired consistency. Some like the puree smooth, others like it chunky. The ingredients should be pureed in several batches depending on the size of the food processor or blender.

Place gazpacho in a large pitcher or glass bowl. Chill until ready to serve.

To Garnish: Place gazpacho in a nice tall wine glass or any desired glass serving bowl. Top with diced peppers, onion and croutons prior to serving.

See photo on page 169

BRIE - TOURNAMENT OF ROSES

Tournament of Roses Brie is quite picturesque Brie with all of the fresh edible flowers. I served this Brie for a New Year's Eve Party. It was a success! Incidentally, it was even more special since it coincided with the Tournament of Roses parade. Edible flowers are available in the herb section of the supermarket such as lavender, marigolds, roses, nasturtiums and pansies. Do not use flowers from your garden unless they have been planted from seeds (this prevents getting any toxic chemicals into the flowers.)

Prep time: 20 min. Serves 6 – 10

Ingredients:

1 (2.2 pound)	Brie wheel
8 ounces	cream cheese, softened
3 cups	edible fresh or dried flowers
1/3 cup	pistachio nuts, halved

Open the Brie wheel and remove from box. Unwrap the Brie without removing the wax paper on the bottom.

Spread cream cheese on top and sides and slowly add the remaining ingredients. Make a circle in the middle of the Brie. Make any pattern desired and place fresh or dried flowers and pistachio nuts on top and sides.

Brie – Tournament of Roses, see recipe on page 167.

AL FRESCO MENU

Gazpacho Andalusia, see recipe on page 166.

HUMMUS BI TAHINI
GARBANZO DIP

Hummus means garbanzo beans in Arabic. This dish can be made the day before or just prior to being served. Garlic can be omitted in this recipe. Stir Tahini before measuring. Lemon juice can be increased according to taste.

Prep time: 10 min. Cook time: 10 min. Serves 4

Ingredients:

1 (14-1/2 ounce)	can garbanzo beans, drained
4-5 tablespoons	Tahini (sesame paste)
2 tablespoons	yogurt
1/4 cup	lemon juice
2 cloves	garlic, peeled and crushed
1 teaspoon	cumin
1/4 teaspoon	allspice
salt and pepper	to taste

Garnish:

1 teaspoon	paprika
1 tablespoon	olive oil

Drain liquid from canned garbanzo beans. Fill can with water, add to garbanzo beans. Bring to boil, reduce heat and simmer for 10 minutes. Let cool. Drain cooking liquid from beans.

In a food processor or blender, add garbanzo, Tahini, yogurt, lemon juice, crushed garlic, cumin, allspice, salt and pepper. Process until consistency is quite smooth.

Remove from food processor and place on a platter. Garnish with paprika. Drizzle with olive oil. Serve with Pita slices or crudités of vegetables.

See photo on page 17

GRANITA LEMONI
LEMON GRANITA

Granita means granular. It is frozen in a steel pan and scraped several times to give the texture of ice crystals. This dessert is quite refreshing on hot summer days. Watermelon granita is delicious. Puree the watermelon to fine consistency and freeze, scrape several times. Place in martini glasses and garnish with lemon slices.

Prep time: 8 hrs. Serves 10

Ingredients:

1 cup	granulated sugar
1/2 cup	water
2 large	lemons, peels only
2 ounces	orange liqueur
2 cups	orange juice
1 cup	fresh lemon juice

Place sugar, water and lemon peel in a heavy saucepan. Stir over low heat until sugar is dissolved, pressing the lemon peel with wooden spoon to extract the aromatic oils. Skim off any froth that comes on the surface.

Boil the syrup for 5 minutes without stirring. Remove when syrup is clear. Let cool and discard the peel. Stir in orange liqueur and orange juice. Pour into a shallow 9-inch cake pan and freeze until set. Scrape into a bowl. Transfer the granita into a food processor bowl and process until fluffy like a cake batter. Return to freezer container cover and freeze until solid. Scrape again and whisk the granita just before serving.

To serve: Pour into tall sorbet glasses and decorate with lemon slices. Granita should be served within a few days to maintain its fresh fruit flavor.

Al Fresco Buffet

Buffet Setting

Table Setting

INDEX

ABOUT JEANETTE

Jeanette started her culinary voyage over 27 years ago. She commenced sharing her culinary talents by conducting cooking classes at major department stores and gourmet cook stores in Southern California. In 1982 at the Robinson's Food Festival in Southern California, Jeanette taught side-by-side with famous chefs and cookbook authors, many of whom are household names today, including Michel Guerard.

Jeanette developed recipes to teach cooking classes for several products in the late 80's including Robot Coupe, Cuisinart, Le Creuset, Revere Signature collections, and Gourment Topf to name a few. She has been featured in several newspapers, cooking magazines, radio, and television shows.

Owning and operating her own catering business for over 25 years, Jeanette has served numerous celebrities in private caterings and events and established herself as a premier chef within the culinary industry. Clients of her catering business included stars and celebrities who appreciated her personal love and understanding of the art of cooking as well as her exceptional attention to their enjoyment.

The culinary art is inane to her, but its application is learned by experience and study. Jeanette spent over three years traveling across Europe to perfect her craft through schooling and study with today's most famous culinary experts.

Jeanette's versatile talents have been expressed in fashion design and her originals were featured in Estee Lauder advertisements when she lived in New York City and owned an exclusive boutique in Manhattan. She has done much in the field of graphic and visual art, but her prime interest has always been haute cuisine and gourmet cooking.

Presently, Jeanette retired from Catering and moved to Northern California. She continues pursuing her passion for teaching cooking classes and remains quite popular among her students. She has kept her classes fun and informative, as she did 27 years ago. Jeanette continues to write a monthly column on a variety of culinary subjects in her local newspaper. Jeanette is also a member of the IACP, the International Association of Culinary Professionals.